NURTURING

THE FLAME

*How to Carry on Your Mission
from Generation to Generation*

TERI FAIRCHILD, RCC

Note: All scripture quotations are taken from the New American Bible, (Canada: World Catholic Press, 1987). Old Testament, July 27, 1970, Revised New Testament, August 27, 1986, and Revised Psalms September 10, 1991.

Note: All quotations from the Catechism of the Catholic Church are from First Image Books Edition published April 1995 (New York: Doubleday, 1994).

Copyright © 2016 Teri Fairchild, RCC All rights reserved.

ISBN: 0692752900
ISBN 13 9780692752906
Library of Congress Control Number: 2016914567 Next Generation Publishing, Dubuque, IA

Introduction

"EACH DAY, 10,000 BABY BOOMERS retire and begin receiving Medicare and Social Security benefits."[i] "To keep your business running if you die or are otherwise incapacitated, a succession plan is vital. But according to a recent report, 66 percent of business owners haven't gotten around to inking one." [ii]

"88% of current family business owners believe the same family or families will control their business in five years, but succession statistics undermine this belief. According to The Family Firm Institute, only about 30% of family and businesses survive into the second generation, 12% are still viable into the third generation, and only about 3% of all family businesses operate into the fourth generation or beyond. There is a disconnect between the optimistic belief of today's family business owners and the reality of the massive failure of family companies to survive through the generations. Research indicates that failures can essentially be traced to one factor: an unfortunate lack of family business succession planning." [iii] During such a critical time in history, it's time to use a proven model for transitioning organizations.

Organizations transitioning from one generation to the next have relied solely on accountants, attorneys, and financial advisers with dismal results. At the same time, the Catholic Church has survived at least fifty generations, if you consider that most business owners have forty year careers. More than two thousand years ago, Jesus handed his apostle Peter the keys to the kingdom. And, through ancient traditions of papal succession (266 popes), the Catholic Church continues to play an essential role in the spiritual lives of millions around the globe.

At the beginning of his three-year ministry, Jesus spent time in the desert reflecting on his mission. He networked to recruit his management team of disciples and communicated the core values of the Church. Jesus conducted seminars in many locations to spread his message. He communicated and implemented the strategic plan for his Church. He developed key performance indicators by way of example with his healings, teachings, and miracles. The disciples spent time with their CEO in leadership training and coaching to achieve their goals. Jesus was clearly a change agent, articulating that his followers would need to lead a new way of life to spread his teachings. Peter was chosen as the next CEO, and when it was time for Jesus to retire, he made the ultimate sacrifice with his crucifixion and death. And finally, to be sure he was leaving behind a sustainable organization; he left the valuable gift of the Holy Spirit to help guide Peter to success in his new role.

Yes, the Catholic Church is a living example of proper succession management and provides a simplified model for business owners and executives to follow in transitioning organizations into the future.

The book you are about to read will show you how Jesus created a simple succession plan for his new organization, the Catholic Church. It will demonstrate how, by using some of the same strategic planning methods used today, he positioned the Catholic Church to last forever. By following the same steps, today's business owner will have the time- tested, proven tools to carry on succession of a family business or organization for years to come.

Table of Contents

Introduction: Three percent of all family businesses are still viable into the fourth generation and beyond. The Catholic Church has survived for at least fifty generations with 266 popes throughout two thousand years. It is a living example of proper succession management. So what better model to follow?

Chapter One How entrepreneurship parallels the three temptations of Jesus in the desert. It's all about the mission - the Church on earth has the same temptations entrepreneurs experience as they build their businesses.

Chapter Two The foundation of any organization is its people. Jesus selected his disciples and outlines best practices of how organizations recruit people. Jesus' inner circle of apostles is much like modern management teams. Without them, the legacy can't be carried.

Chapter Three Core values provide a behavioral foundation for all members of an organization. Human virtues are firm attitudes, stable dispositions, and habitual perfections of intellect and will that govern our actions, order our passions, and guide our conduct according to faith and reason. Core purpose answers the question, "Why are we here?"

Chapter Four Continuous improvement meetings help businesses identify strategies for leaders and helps set priorities for the next three to five years. These strategies are called key targets. Just as Jesus implemented his key targets during his three-year ministry, it's important for business owners to execute a plan from the beginning.

Chapter Five Measurement of performance and processes are vital. Jesus and the Church consistently evaluate the success of the mission.

Chapter Six Jesus handed Peter the keys to the kingdom. Learn best practices for selecting the next CEO and how we can learn the best selection process from Jesus.

Chapter Seven The transition process is crucial. Both the transition to leader and to Christian require an internal transformation to create a new beginning.

Chapter Eight: High potential employees need additional skills to be successful in their new roles as leaders. Determine important development competencies for new leaders. As the ultimate leader, Jesus prepared his disciples to carry out his mission for the Church.

Chapter Nine Most CEOs, entrepreneurs, and leaders experience a sense of loss in leaving an organization. Jesus made a profound sacrifice with his death but also signifies great hope with his resurrection. There is another chapter for all of us.

Chapter Ten The Church was left with the Holy Spirit and many other gifts for Catholics. This chapter outlines those gifts and highlights how outgoing leaders can serve as valuable resources.

Conclusion The succession process to transition an organization into the future is similar to succession through Jesus - the steps Jesus took to start the Church. See how others have succeeded by following the story that has stood the test of time.

Acknowledgments

I WOULD LIKE TO THANK my parents, Del and Mary Ament, for teaching me the importance of faith. This book would not have been written without the living example of their faith and their decision to bring me up in the Catholic Tradition. I thank my husband Riley for his love and inexhaustible gift of patience while I was writing this book. I also appreciate the support and encouragement from my family. I would like to credit the members of the Citywide Bible Study Group in Dubuque, IA for organizing the ongoing programs from The Great Adventure Catholic Bible Study Programs from Ascension Press. These programs taught me how to articulate my faith. The New American Bible and Catechism of the Catholic Church have been invaluable resources to help me present an accurate presentation of Catholic Church teachings. In addition, I would like to thank all the wonderful business writers and resources for their respective insights that I've been able to reference in this book.

Writing a book is a daunting process. I would not have been able to complete this project without my dream team of editors and artist. Thank you to Dan McCarthy, Valerie Kramer, and the editors at CreateSpace. Also, a big thank you goes to Paula Keck for capturing the tone and contents of the book in the cover design and graphics.

A big thank you on this project goes to Kim Hesprich. Without her help, this book would not be in print. Her vast biblical knowledge, attention to detail, fortitude and encouragement provided the direction I needed to pull the concepts in this book together. I appreciate how much she cares about the message.

Most importantly, I want to thank God for all His blessings in my life. It's an honor and privilege to share this message.

CHAPTER 1

Entrepreneur Desert Exile

BEFORE JESUS DEPARTS ON HIS new mission, the Church on earth, he confronts three temptations. These are the same temptations entrepreneurs experience when embarking on the journeys of their businesses.

The Temptation of Jesus
At once the Spirit drove him out into the desert,
and he remained in the desert for forty days, tempted by Satan.
He was among wild beasts, and the angels ministered to him.
Mark 1:12-13

Starting a business venture can seem like you are among wild beasts wrought with temptation.

Bishop Robert Barron captures the importance of trials in his 2016 Ash Wednesday edition of "Lenten Reflections": "In so many of the great figures of salvation history Abraham, Jacob, Joseph, Moses, Isaiah, Jeremiah, David, etc. - a period of testing or trial is required before they can commence their work... This was the purpose of Jesus's forty-day sojourn in the desert, which we model during Lent. The desert represents a stripping away of our attachments, so as to make the fundamental things appear. In the desert, there are no distractions or diversions or secondary matters. Everything is basic, necessary, and simple. Either one survives or one doesn't. One finds in the desert strengths and weaknesses he never knew he had." [iv]

The same is true for entrepreneurs. Starting any new venture is like entering the desert. Trials like being socially ostracized for taking a risk and leaving long standing work relationships to create something new can be lonely. Since most businesses take at least three years to show a profit, it's basic survival.

The Temptation for Worldly Pleasures

When Jesus was tempted in the desert, the first temptation from Satan was for worldly pleasures. After fasting forty days, Jesus was hungry. He was tempted to satisfy his physical needs over the good of God's will.

Jesus knew that his mission was from God and for God. He didn't measure the success of his mission based on satisfying his worldly pleasures. He based it only on carrying out the will of his Father.

My Desert Experience

When I was a little girl, I remember my mom counting her egg money. Neighbors routinely came to the door and purchased a few dozen eggs. Mom would collect the money and put it in a small envelope. It was a nice little side business that supplemented the income generated from the family farm. That egg money probably paid for a lot of the family groceries when my parents were first starting out. Mom and Dad were entrepreneurs, and it wasn't always easy.

The youngest of six girls raised on a family farm in Northwest Iowa, I was witness to many struggles. There were hot summer days of helping in the dirty fields—pulling itchy weeds and wiping the sweat from my forehead—when it was supposed to be summer vacation. And when the rain just wouldn't seem to fall for weeks, we felt the angst from Mom and Dad. Everyone in the family made sacrifices to make ends meet. My parents preached and practiced the virtue of getting rid of debt as soon as you could. They worked together and constantly discussed a personal financial strategy. They were good business people.

The office was in our farmhouse. I can still remember walking by the office as a child when Mom and Dad were talking. Mother would be outlining an idea to buy more hogs or sell some grain at a certain price. Together, they made good business decisions as entrepreneurs. They practiced many of Dave Ramsey's steps before he became a well-known expert. Dave Ramsey is a personal money management expert and popular national radio personality. He teaches people how to be responsible with their money and acquire enough wealth to take care of loved ones, retire with dignity, and give generously to others.

Now, I'm the entrepreneur. After sixteen years in the newspaper industry as a salesperson and sales manager, I started my first business venture serving as area manager for a professional development franchise. In 2002, I took over a territory in Eastern Iowa so I could teach the leadership and management methods that had a significant effect on my career.

Now, as the owner of a business coaching organization, I provide tools and inspiration to people and organizations in transition. Specifically, I help businesses with succession management.

As a former sales manager and entrepreneur, the temptation for worldly pleasure has always been a challenging concept for me. I have focused on top-line revenue for companies throughout my entire career. Salespeople are generally motivated by money—and I'm no exception. Entrepreneurs are typically responsible for making sure there is enough money in the revenue bucket for reinvestment into the company, payroll, and budgeted expenses. Failure is not an option. Managing cash flow requires a focus on investing dollars only on critical areas basic to building a foundation for the business, with little cash left over for pleasure.

In the early days of my second entrepreneurial effort, I was tempted at times to connect with a recruiting firm to just "see what was out there" in terms of sales management jobs. When I wasn't clear on my brand or what products to offer, when I had doubts, it seemed like a good idea to keep my options open. I would tell myself I could keep working on the business, and if by some stroke of good fortune, I landed some lucrative corporate job, well, then, all the better. I kept an eye out for sales and marketing jobs for the first six to twelve months. It's tempting to walk two paths.

It's difficult to stay focused on your mission when you aren't reaping the rewards you're used to having when someone else is signing your paycheck! You have to watch every penny spent and cut back on some of the luxuries. I took new clothes, lawn care, and nice vacations for granted. Jesus was focused on his mission and not tempted by Satan for worldly pleasures. Through his strength, I overcame the temptation to check out the help wanted ads and kept my mission at the forefront.

The lowest point of ramping up my coaching business was in February 2013. The previous year, I had hired a company to help with attraction marketing. I have a college degree in marketing and believe most businesses need an inbound and outbound marketing strategy. While this company got me up to speed on a lot of the new technologies used in marketing today, they did not succeed in generating many leads. I found my business headed toward debt. I had made a commitment to my husband, Riley, that I would not be going into a lot of debt with this venture. All those Dave Ramsey videos started playing in my head.

At that same time, my sister Jill passed away unexpectedly at age fifty-four. I was heartbroken. This was definitely not an easy time to get excited about anything, much less selling. I faced a lot of rejection with sales calls, and my confidence was bottoming out.

During that time I had a better sense of where I should position my brand and product offerings. I spent a great deal of time creating my leadership development program. The program was designed based on the best practices in business and is delivered as both training and coaching, which is unique to most professional development programs. It turned out to be a great decision, but I wasn't able to deliver many services while simultaneously developing the product, so revenue was dismal to say the least.

As we were deciding what to put on my sister's tombstone, we found that she had this scripture taped to her computer: "Then the Lord will guide you always and give you plenty even on the parched land" (Isaiah 58:11). I taped it to my computer to remind me of my sister, and it has helped me get through the more challenging times in my business. Jesus resisted temptations from the devil by quoting scripture. Referring to scripture during times of temptation seemed to work well for me, too.

THE TEMPTATION FOR POWER

Jesus was tempted in a second way with power. Satan tempted Jesus to use his messianic authority to gain worldly power, to become a king. Jesus replied, "The Lord, your God, shall you worship and him alone shall you serve" (Matthew 4:10).

The early days of any new venture are uncertain. You have to have the fortitude and belief that you will make it, and you are typically earning substantially less income than you did in your previous position.

When I first started my business, I kept a journal. Reading over those writings now is quite telling. As I navigated the decisions that would decide my major products, there were many ups and downs. One day, I would be on top of the world because I had landed a great sale and knew I would have cash to get me through another couple of months. The next entry would outline a huge, gut-wrenching setback. It was a roller coaster ride, for sure!

> I take three steps forward and two steps back. I am working on the Registered Corporate Coach™ designation, and have six hours of coaching completed. Last week, I did my final interview with (Company X), but I still don't know what they are going to do with the position. I am actively involved in a proposal for (Company Y) and am super psyched about that project. I also have a proposal I'm working on for (Company Z). I also have three possibilities for coaching clients. LOTS OF BALLS IN THE AIR! I need to get some closure on all this so I know what to work on. This level of uncertainty is very unsettling, but at least I have a number of prospects out there. I just need to hang in there and keep moving forward.
>
> October 11, 2011 Journal Entry

While I landed some great clients in the first few years of my business from 2011 through 2012, I had to reinvest a lot in the business. I am lucky my husband was a Dave Ramsey fan when I started my second entrepreneurial venture. Since we had already been through this once before with my initial seven-year experience with the professional development franchise, he knew the beginning of this venture would be difficult, but with patience, we would get back to a decent lifestyle as I gained momentum.

However, this second round of tackling the American dream was a bit more challenging. I had to establish my own brand this time. It was 100 percent me. And I was almost ten years older. With the professional development franchise, it wasn't rare that I would get up at 4:00 a.m. and travel sixty-five miles to begin instructing by 7:00 a.m., teach a class until noon, sell all afternoon, and prepare for an evening class from 6:00 to 9:30 p.m., then finally arrive home around 10:00 p.m. For this second entrepreneurial venture, at fifty years old, I didn't have the energy or desire to work morning, noon, and night.

I remember a period of time when I was being swept into the new age culture. I was seeking something different than what I thought the traditional Catholic Mass offered. The Eastern religions were so interesting, and I even found horoscopes fascinating. I have always been intrigued with the differences in people, and I love learning about the astrological signs how Leos are attracted to Sagittarians and why Libras are the quiet ones. When visiting Chinese restaurants, I paid particular attention to the whole system of Chinese astrology. Part of me knew this was not consistent with the teachings of the Catholic faith, but I was just curious. I remember buying a number of books and building quite a library. But the more I learned, the more I began living a life of unfaithfulness. On one hand, I never stopped practicing my Catholic faith, but on the other, I was reading horoscopes to give me "insight" to predict the future.

In 2008, my husband, Riley, and I attended a mission at our Catholic Church, and the missionary priest clearly and directly denounced these practices as inconsistent with Catholicism. Like Jesus, I had been tempted to an easier way for worldly power. I had failed where he had prevailed.

I was ashamed that I had allowed myself to get roped into serving two masters. I went home and immediately threw all my horoscope books in the trash. Looking back, I think it was a need for security that caused me to get into the new age stuff. As an entrepreneur and salesperson, you never know where your next sale will come from, which causes uncertainty. I craved the security of knowing what would happen as astrology portends to provide. I stopped depending on God.

The Temptation for Glory

Jesus' third temptation was for glory. This was the temptation for Jesus to put himself before God. Jesus did not give in to the temptation for glory and consistently listened and sought to do the will of his father.

Fear of failure is another area in which I have been continually tested. When I made the decision to open my business, I consciously decided to bank on my own abilities. I put all my eggs in one basket, me, in the belief that I could make the right decisions to build and maintain a successful business, which can be very tense and humbling. I emphasize the word humbling here, as the trait of humility is crucial to one's growth as an entrepreneur. Let me share an experience.

I fondly remember my years working with the professional development franchise. I learned best practices in public speaking, sales, leadership, and presentation methodology. Most of all, I learned to be humble. If I had not learned this trait, I would never have learned all the things I did.

The culture of the franchise organization is heavily focused on standardized presentation. As an instructor, I felt an overwhelming obligation to deliver the classroom material at a very high standard. During the instructor candidate programs, the master trainers teach you to uphold this standard. I remember feeling almost insulted at first. At certification events, the master trainers would interrupt you over and over again and have you say things differently. They'd say, "Try this." "Start over." "Smile, you're cutting off part of the room, open up your body." And on and on. Didn't these people know that I was an accomplished professional? Becoming vulnerable and open to accepting the teaching and learning of the new skills made me feel very uncomfortable.

Over time I learned to accept the coaching and stopped questioning why they wanted me to "distribute the ballots" instead of "pass out the ballots." They didn't care. They wanted it done their way, insisting on the delivery of a polished, professional, and yes, standardized program.

So when the time came for me to deliver my first professional development program on my own, I was terrified. It was a twelve week program and contained a lot of memorized language. I was so afraid I would draw a blank in the middle of class and forget what to do next. The first night of the first session, I was sick to my stomach. During the first part of the class, I asked all the participants to stand up and shake hands with the other members of the class. I opened the class and blurted out, "Okay, let's all shake hands," entirely omitting the language I had been taught to explain the rationale behind the shaking of hands. I immediately ducked behind the flip chart and had an anxiety attack, but then I had a little chat with myself to the effect of "Okay, Teri, pull yourself together!" It was brutal.

I did get the memorized language down and eventually became a decent instructor. My husband, Riley, was relieved. When I first began teaching the program, he'd say, "Is there something wrong with you? You seem uptight." Then he'd pause and say, "Oh that's right, you have class tonight. You're always edgy on the nights you have to teach." I was so relieved when I became proficient enough to teach the program their way, and those feelings of high anxiety went away.

The point is that you have to take the coaching in order to get better. You have to be humble. You have to get low. Take a dip. I remember a number of instructor candidates who were retired and seeking second careers. In the past, a few had high-level corporate positions that required them to assume a dominant leadership role. Some of these men and women wouldn't accept the coaching from the master trainers, and as a result, didn't get better and never made it into the classroom. They couldn't get humble.

What I learned over time was that the really outstanding instructors weren't focused on themselves or their delivery; they remained engaged with classroom participants and their main interest was in helping participants stretch outside their comfort zones to live life intentionally.

Jesus resisted the temptation for glory and stayed focused on serving God. As he prepared for his mission, he spent forty days in the desert with his coach. Starting any new mission is like that. It requires humility to say, "I have to spend some time to learn this new thing and put enough hours into it to achieve mastery." It also helps for us to keep in mind why what we are doing allows us to serve God.

Summary

Businesses need to make money but avoid the temptation for worldly pleasures. Entrepreneurs must deliver value to stakeholders but avoid the temptation for power. Leaders need to learn skills to build the organization while maintaining humility and do their work for the glory of God.

The building of any mission starts with preparation and trial. The foundation is built on the belief or purpose of the mission. Having dealt with these three temptations, Jesus was ready for his mission. He is the ultimate role model for entrepreneurs, and his examples of overcoming temptation in the desert help us as followers to stay on the right track.

Chapter One Highlights

1. Desert experiences resemble basic survival.
2. Uncertainty is common.
3. Learning new skills requires humility.

Reflection Question: What are your biggest challenges as an entrepreneur or organization leader?

Action Step: How will you manage uncertainty and demonstrate humility?

Jesus went into the desert to prepare for his mission, where he experienced three temptations:
1. Worldly pleasure – To satisfy his physical needs over the good of God's will.
2. Power – To become a king.
3. Glory – To put himself before God.

Reflection Question: In what ways are you being tempted?

Action Step: What will you do to overcome the temptations you face?

CHAPTER 2

Building a Team

THE FOUNDATION OF ANY ORGANIZATION is its people. This chapter covers how Jesus selected his disciples and the best practices of recruitment. It also compares Jesus' inner circle of apostles with today's modern management teams.

The Call of the First Disciples
As he passed by the Sea of Galilee,
he saw Simon and his brother Andrew
casting their nets into the sea;
they were fisherman. Jesus said to them,
"Come after me, and I will make you fishers of men."
Mark 1:16 -17

Jesus created a team for his mission on earth, the Church, from a diverse group of ordinary men with different talents. They became the foundation of the Church. The twelve apostles were composed of a variety of personalities. Not one of them was a rabbi or scholar, nor did they possess any extraordinary skills. Peter and Andrew were brothers, as were James and John, the two sons of Zebedee; all were simple fishermen. Peter was quick to speak and the most extreme of the Twelve in his impulsive nature. Andrew would have been identified as a modern day connector. According to Malcolm Gladwell's *The Tipping Point*, "Connectors know lots of people. They are the kinds of people who know everyone."[v] Andrew was a connector and introduced his brother Simon (Peter) to Jesus.

James, known as James the Greater could be intense. John was probably in his teens when he met Jesus. He was the youngest disciple and the only one with Jesus at the foot of the cross during his crucifixion. John is referred to as the apostle that Jesus loved. Philip was practical and stubborn at times. Jesus referred to Nathanial as a real Israelite. Sometimes called Bartholomew, he could be cynical. Matthew left his life as a wealthy and dishonest tax collector to take on a new identity and is known for writing the Gospel of Matthew. Thomas had a questioning mind and is best known as the "doubter." James the Less is known for his obscurity. Simon the Zealot was a political fanatic who traded a struggle against Rome for a struggle against sin. Thaddeus is characterized as a tenderhearted, gentle man who displayed childlike humility. And finally, Judas was the treasurer, best known for betraying Jesus for thirty pieces of silver.

"As he passed by the Sea of Galilee, he saw Simon and his brother Andrew casting their nets into the sea; they were fishermen" (Mark 1:16). Jesus was out and about. Great recruiters are always out and about, making connections in the world.

While Jesus has the ability to see into our hearts, statistics indicate that most organizations need other best practices to assemble a team that will successfully continue its mission into the future long after the team members are out of the picture.

MY TEAM BUILDING EXPERIENCES

I received an e-mail from Jennifer. She said she was losing her job at a large national calling center because the company was closing the office and was interested in learning more about opportunities at my professional development franchise. I reviewed her resume and responded by asking her to lunch.

Jennifer made a very good first impression; she was friendly and professional. During our luncheon interview, she indicated that she had been a part of a professional development program as a high school student and had a life-changing experience. Working for this particular professional development franchise would be her dream job.

How could I not pursue her? I was just at the point in my business when I was ready to hire a sales representative, so I was interested, although cautious. I had dozens of fresh-faced, enthusiastic people tell me how excited they were about a selling opportunity, only to crash and burn in the real world of selling. You could say I'm a little skeptical when hiring sales reps.

During my days at the newspaper, I remember having to fire under-performing sales reps, and it was the worst part of my job. Managing was a real chore when you had to put a rep whose performance was marginal on a ninety-day performance-improvement plan. With this task, I had to write a list of specific activities that the underperforming rep needed to complete, which were the basic duties of the position. The improvement plan included a note at the bottom, indicating that termination might be in order if any of these activities were not completed.

There was not a single situation in which a rep came out on top, and, alas, they were all terminated. Sometimes they would lie about seeing accounts, and at other times they just refused to make sales calls. One particular sales rep never had a deal going. She was consistently negative. When I asked her what was going on with an account, she would grunt back, "They aren't doing anything." After she left a few months later, I learned she was going home every afternoon to take a nap! I have to admit, it is really hard to sell stuff when you are sleeping.

In one situation, I felt just awful. The rep just couldn't ramp up to the demands of the position. I came home in tears the night she was terminated from her position. Right then and there I decided I needed to do a better job of selecting people who could meet the demands and be successful in their particular roles. So when I saw a flyer come across my desk from an assess-ment company, I was intrigued. The sales rep from the company called and asked if I wanted a demonstration of the product. It was then that I learned the concepts and benefits of psychometric profiling tools.

So when Jennifer came along, I had quite a bit of experience in hiring and using assessments to get a better understanding of "job fit" in hiring for sales positions. It was a win-win for both of us. Jennifer's customer service background made me nervous. I had not had good luck with people moving from service to sales. Another red flag was her lack of a college degree, although she had a couple of years of community college and during the interview expressed an interest in going back and finishing school. I think she was even getting some funds for college from her current company as a result of the office closure. These concerns made me very deliberate in my hiring process. My next step was to have her complete a few assessments. I sent her an invitation to complete a couple of different assessments online that would provide me both positive and negative information on how she might perform in her role as a sales representative and trainer. Her ego strength or resilience was well below the preferred range. Basically, this meant that when she had a setback or lost a sale, she would have a difficult time bouncing back from that rejection or setback. Jennifer did score high in sociability and accommodation, which was good, because people with high scores in sociability find it easy to make connections. They love to be around people and make friends. The downside was that she might find it lonely working in an office by herself as she would be required to do in the role of a professional development sales representative.

She might also have the potential to be a professional visitor, the kind of rep who made a lot of sales calls but couldn't close the sale. Sales reps with high accommodation scores also have a tendency to be uncomfortable in handling objections. They tend to cut their prices quickly when challenged and discount products unnecessarily to justify their sales, and they don't like to ask for money on past due accounts. They have a tough time handling the interaction of difficult people and, worse yet, find it stressful dealing with customer problems.

On the bright side, Jennifer had above-average verbal skills, which would help her to communicate as an instructor. She had a moderate amount of energy and assertiveness to help her with the multitasking that a sales position often requires and the drive to keep prospecting. Finally, she had a high independence score. Since she would be working in a remote office, it was essential that she work independently and run her territory as though it was her own business. Her interests also indicated she was a perfect match in the interest category for the position. She was interested in activities of persuasiveness and presentation of ideas; helping people; and being imaginative, original, and artistic. These three occupational interests were a 92 percent match to those created for the professional development sales position: enterprising, people service, and creative.

After serious consideration, I made the decision to hire her, but I went in with my eyes wide open. The assessment reports were a great coaching tool. When Jennifer lost a sale, I would nonchalantly encourage her: "It's no big deal. Move on. There are other fish in the sea." She learned to manage her high sociability by doing a lot of networking and presenting. She was very motivated to be a trainer and was an excellent presenter, so every time she lined up a speaking engagement, it was like making thirty or forty sales calls instead of one. Jennifer's public speaking turned out to be a great strategy for her to build the business. In terms of her high accommodation behavior, I had to do a lot of directive coaching: that is, be specific and direct in my approach when it came to collections and getting her to pick up the phone rather than using e-mail to handle conflicts.

During the five years she worked for me, Jennifer completed her college degree and became a consistent, award-winning salesperson for the company. She had a great attitude, worked hard, and was a blessing to work with. A key member of my team, she was responsible for generating a significant share of the revenue and delivering the corresponding services in our territory. I feel strongly the assessments were the key to providing the insights I needed to coach her to her top potential and help her through some difficult times in her career. Jennifer is an example of an ordinary person who ended up being an extraordinary producer and loyal advocate of the professional development competencies she was teaching.

Other team members contributed in their own way. I was fortunate to have a very quiet, loyal and supportive administrative assistant. She worked for me in the evenings out of her home and had a full-time position during the day. We communicated by phone, fax and mail. She was extremely supportive; we never spoke an unkind word to each other, and she continually asked what she could do to better serve the company.

I also had a few avocational instructors who taught for me. One in particular had excellent speaking skills and was a godsend to me when I was suffering from burnout building the business and maintaining an arduous teaching schedule. His convictions were strong as was the approach he used. I appreciated his intellectual side and sense of humor.

We were all very different people who together helped build a successful and thriving territory. The thing we had in common was our positive experience in the professional development classroom. We were centered on the mission to deliver the same value we received from our experience to others. We all shared the same mission

SUCCESSION PLANNING FOR CRITICAL ROLES

Assessment tools are used to help organizations select and develop high potential employees in succession management today. According to *The Executive's Guide to Succession Planning*, written by Profiles International, LLC, "the first step in succession planning is identifying the critical positions in your company." [vi] (Profiles International was acquired by John Wiley & Sons in 2014). Critical roles are typically the positions in the inner circle or management of the company or key roles the organization can't do without. Some organizations call them the management team. I recall a time during my ad sales days when I was holding a meeting with some key employees on my advertising team. My boss walked in and said, "I can see this is a meeting of the brain trust." I thought that was clever. Whatever the term your organization uses - "top management," "executive team," "brain trust," or "the council" these are the critical positions, those that Profiles International, LLC believes "organizations simply cannot function without. What would happen if they left? "[vii] Are they the only people in the organization who can fulfill those roles? If so, the organization is very vulnerable.

The same goes for middle managers; some are probably nearing retirement age and will need to be replaced in the near future. Find out what makes these people special and essential, and you can find similar attributes in other employees. Knowing the key roles in an organization is the obvious first step toward succession management.

Jesus had an inner circle in his organization. Only three of his disciples, Peter, James, and John, were permitted to witness the raising of the daughter of Jairus. "He did not allow anyone to accompany him inside except Peter, James, and John, the brother of James" (Mark 5:37). It was only Peter, James, and John who witnessed the Transfiguration. "After six days Jesus took Peter, James, and

John his brother, and led them up a high mountain by themselves. And he was transfigured before them; his face shone like the sun and his clothes became white as light" (Matthew 17:1-2). "Then Jesus came with them to a place called Gethsemane, and he said to his disciples, 'Sit here while I go over there and pray.' He took along Peter and the two sons of Zebedee, and began to feel sorrow and distress" (Matthew 26:36-37). Among the twelve disciples, Jesus only allowed three of them into his inner circle.

Just like most teams, the three had challenging aspects to their behavior. Impulsive and emotional, Peter often spoke before he thought. Rash in word and act alike, he was full of zeal and enthusiasm. Peter was the first to get out of the boat and follow Jesus when he walked on the water. When he started to falter, he pleaded, "Lord, save me!" (Matthew 14:30). He was also the apostle who struck the high priest's servant, cutting off his ear as Jesus was being arrested. Peter quickly emerged a leader among the disciples.

James was called the "son of thunder." On June 21, 2006, the Catholic News Agency reported, "Pope Benedict teaches about James, the 'son of thunder,' the name that Jesus gave to James, perhaps refers 'to his impetuous zeal,' said the Holy Father, a characteristic the Apostle showed, among other occasions, when he wished to bid fire come down from heaven to consume a village of the Samaritans that had refused to receive the Lord. His reaction, Pope Benedict explained, 'clearly showed his love for Jesus, but probably also expressed the traditional enmity between Jews and Samaritans.' But, the Holy Father continued, Jesus had no love for violence."[viii] John was also known to have a fiery temperament with a larger than life personality.

And just like most management team members who rise through the ranks, James and John were ambitious too. Their mother asked for a higher place in heaven for them. "Then the mother of the sons of Zebedee approached him with her sons and did him homage, wishing to ask him for something, he said to her, 'What do you wish?' She answered him, 'Command that these two sons of mine sit, one at your right and the other at your left, in your kingdom.' Jesus said in reply, 'You do not know what you are asking. Can you drink the cup I am going to drink?' They said to him, 'We can.' He replied, 'My cup you will indeed drink, but to sit at my right and at my left [, this] is not mine to give but is for those whom it has been prepared by my Father.' When the ten heard this, they became indignant at the two brothers" (Matthew 20:20-24).

What? Competition and squabbling among the management team members? Does this sound familiar?

Hiring Statistics

"According to a study by Leadership IQ, 46% of newly hired employees will fail within 18 months, while only 19% will achieve unequivocal success. But contrary to popular belief, technical skills are not the primary reason why new hires fail; instead, poor interpersonal skills dominate the list, flaws which many of their managers admit were overlooked during the job interview process."[ix] That's why the use of assessments, or psychometric profiling tools, in selecting the right people for critical roles in a company is so important. A comprehensive selection tool will give you information about the total person. Based on identifying innate personality traits, abilities, and behaviors, assessing for job fit determines if a person CAN do a job, HOW they will do a job, and if they will ENJOY the job. Every human being is motivated and driven by different influences. Job fit outlines the unique job related qualities that make a person productive.

THREE-LEGGED STOOL APPROACH

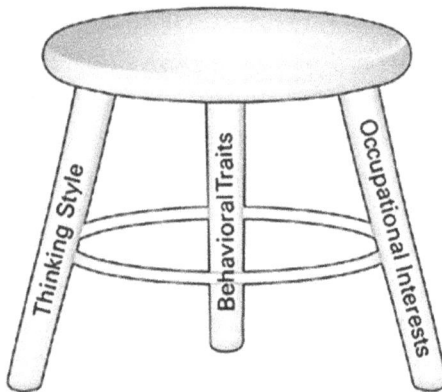

Job fit is composed of three areas and can be explained using a three-legged stool concept:

1. **Thinking style** - This measures whether a potential candidate can deal with the mental demands of a position. It's composed of verbal skill and reasoning and numeric skill and reasoning. CAN they do the job?

2. **Behavioral traits** - This measures whether a candidate will be comfortable with the environment and the people they must work with. HOW will they do the job?

3. **Occupational interests** - This measures whether the candidate will enjoy the work and be motivated to do it. Do they WANT to do the job?

Throughout my career, the use of assessments has allowed me to hire candidates who are likely to succeed, coach them to success, and understand the differences in their learning styles, behavioral characteristics, motivations, and interests.

Without a formal process for selection, many organizations are vulnerable to confirmation bias. According to Psychology Today, "Confirmation bias occurs from the direct influence of desire on beliefs. When people would like a certain idea/concept to be true, they end up believing it to be true. They are motivated by wishful thinking. This error leads the individual to stop gathering information when the evidence gathered so far confirms the views (prejudices) one would like to be true."[x]

The same thing happens in the interviewing process when it comes to first impressions. If our first impression of a candidate is positive, we are subconsciously biased and will gather evidence to support that first impression. The opposite is also true. If the candidate makes a bad first impression, we might gather evidence to support why that candidate is not a good fit for the position or the company.

Many organizations rely on top executives who believe they have a feel or special knack for candidate selection. The story begins with a supposed rock-star quality candidate being hired for a management-level position based on the "good feelings" or "gut instinct" of the CEO. The CEO is impressed by this candidate's ambitious nature, and the candidate is subsequently hired for the open management position. After a short time, it's clear that most of the new manager's peers do not hold this individual in the same high regard as the CEO. As a matter of fact, there is a widely held belief that most of his management peers would be willing to "pay big money to see the person taken out to the wood shed for a beating." Shortly after, that same rock star manager is no longer with the organization.

The Society for Human Resources Management (SHRM) *Foundation's Retaining Talent: A Guide to Analyzing and Managing Employee Turnover,* part of its Effective Practice Guidelines Series, points out, "Employee departures cost a company time, money, and other resources. Research suggests that direct replacement costs can reach as high as 50%-60% of an employee's annual salary, with total costs associated with turnover ranging from 90% to 200% of annual salary." [xi]

IDENTIFYING TOP PERFORMERS

The best way to avoid failure is to study the people who have demonstrated a high level of success in a position. This success is referred to as high job fit, and top performers typically have a high percentage of job fit.

When I work with organizations, I ask about critical positions. I ask the CEO, "Who do you have in these roles now who are top performers? Are there top performers in one or many of the critical positions in the organization?" Once we identify the top performers for each role, we send them an invitation to complete an assessment that asks a series of questions. Hiring managers or HR administrators simply forward a link. The assessment does not need to be monitored, so the candidate can complete it from any computer with Internet access. The system instantly scores the assessments and informs the hiring managers where they can access the results.

After the top performer completes the assessment, we review the results with the boss. He or she is always amazed at the accuracy of the data and quickly sees the value of creating a performance model based on that top performer. Organizations are advised to develop top-performance models based on the top performer data. We then use that model as a guide to recruit and select new people for that role. Once these performance models are established, organizations deliver the assessments to their internal and external candidates through the Internet. The hiring manager uses the data from each applicant to assist in the interviewing, selection, and onboarding process.

Essentially, a comprehensive assessment to assess job fit answers three questions: First, can the candidate meet the mental demands of the position? Second, do the candidate's behavioral traits compare favorably to those of a top performer in the same role? Finally, does the candidate have interests that align with the position requirements? The assessment provides a comprehensive look at a candidate and allows employers to hire candidates with their eyes wide open.

There are many types of psychometric profiling tools available on the market, and I've sampled many of them. Be sure any assessment that's used for selection during the hiring process is used consistently among applicants and meets or exceeds the ADA, EEOC, Department of Labor standards for educational and psychological testing, Title 1 of the Civil Rights Act of 1964, and Uniform Guidelines for Employee Selection Procedures requirements. Results from an assessment should only be used as one-third of the decision making when making a hire. We'll discuss this more in-depth in chapter six.

EMPLOYEE DEVELOPMENT

Savvy managers continue to use the results of the selection assessment tools they used to select the employee to coach the employee. What are the areas outside the performance model in which the employee might need help in adapting, especially in the behavioral categories? Will the employee need to stretch outside his or her comfort zone to be more social? Will the individual need help with decision-making? Will he or she need help keeping things in perspective when under stress? Coaching reports are an invaluable tool to use with employees throughout their tenure with the manager or company.

A high-performing assessment tool will help to engage an employee throughout the life cycle of his or her employment with an organization. It is a valuable tool for human resources and managers to select the best candidate for a position by understanding how a candidate matches the performance model of a position. By understanding the new hire's cognitive style, it's also helpful for developing a customized training program for onboarding. Finally, it provides a tool for coaching employees to success with a strong understanding of their behavioral traits. Decisions about getting an employee involved in specific company projects based on their occupational interests is also a possibility for managers who *intentionally* use the information in selection and coaching reports.

EMPLOYEE ENGAGEMENT

Though the apostles displayed many human frailties, the three also exhibited loyalty to Jesus and his mission. Peter became the rock, a fearless missionary for the Church. James endured hardship and persecution. He was the first of Jesus' apostles to be martyred. John, the disciple whom Jesus loved, was especially loyal to Jesus. He is credited with writing five books in the New Testament. Jesus' management team had faith in him; they had courage and were steadfast in their service to the mission of the Church.

Statistics would indicate, however, that most employees are not exhibiting this kind of engagement. According to a Los Angeles Times article headlined "Most workers hate their jobs or have "checked out," Gallup says:

> 7 out of 10 workers have "checked out" at work or are "actively disengaged," according to a recent Gallup survey... The survey classifies three types of employees among the 100 million people in America who hold full time jobs. The first is actively engaged, which represents about 30 million workers. The second type of worker is "not engaged," which accounts for 50 million. These employees are going through the motions at work. The third type, labeled "actively disengaged," hates going to work. These workers - about 20 million - undermine their companies with their attitude, according to the report... Gallup estimates that workers who are actively disengaged cost the U.S. as much as $550 billion in economic activity yearly. [xii]

What's the key to getting more people actively engaged? In addition to the use of a credible selection and coaching tool, another tool I continue to use in my business today to help build engagement and teamwork is the Gallup StrengthsFinder 2.0 assessment. "Based on a 4-year study of human strengths, the Gallup organization created a language of the 34 most common talents and developed the Clifton StrengthsFinder assessment to help people discover and describe these talents."[xiii]

When I conduct a strengths audit with a team I'm working with, a best practice has been to see how balanced the team is in each of the four strength domains: executing, influencing, relationship building and strategic planning. During team-building meetings, participants learn that instead of one dominant leader who tries to do everything or individuals who all have similar strengths, contributions from all four domains lead to a strong and cohesive team.

PERFECTLY BALANCED TEAM

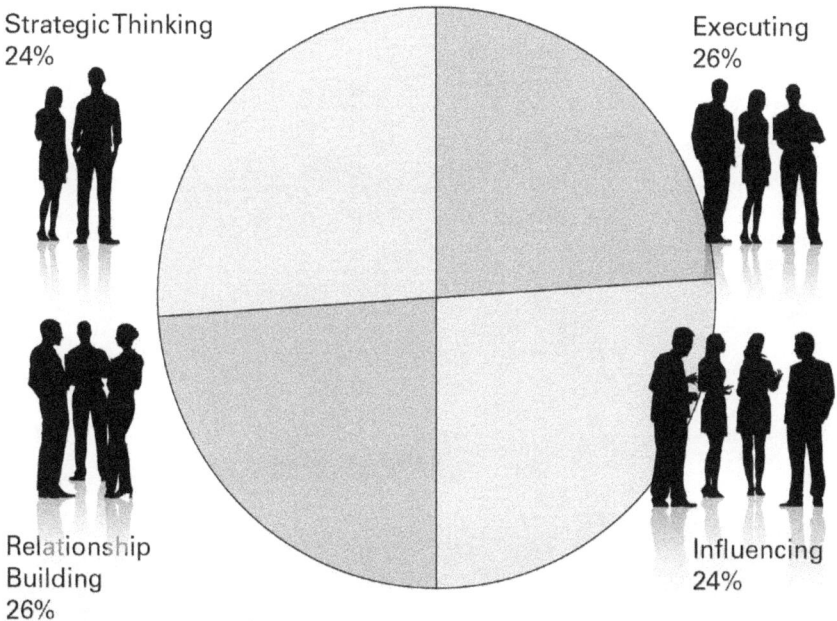

Strategic Thinking 24%

Executing 26%

Relationship Building 26%

Influencing 24%

And while Gallup's Clifton StrengthsFinder is an excellent tool for team building, it's important to acknowledge that Clifton StrengthsFinder is not validated as a selection/hiring tool under the Uniform Guidelines promulgated by the EEOC, and as such, the Clifton StrengthsFinder should not be used as a hiring tool or for selection purposes.

So whether the goal is to select the right people for the organization or to get them to work together productively, the key is individualization. According to Gallup, people especially talented in the individualization theme are "intrigued with the unique qualities of each person. They have a gift for determining how people who are different can work together productively." [xiv]

In this chapter we have discussed a variety of psychometric profiling tools that allow organizations to get below the surface and understand the people who will be responsible for carrying out the mission.

Jesus recruited a diverse team of disciples with varied traits and characteristics. They were all able to apply their talents and gifts in unique ways to build his Church. He brought Peter, James, and John into his inner circle, and they each had critical roles with higher-level responsibilities. They worked to carry out the mission of the Church together.

CHAPTER TWO HIGHLIGHTS

1. About 46 percent of new hires fail within eighteen months.

2. A comprehensive psychometric profiling tool measures thinking style, behavioral traits, and occupational interests of selection candidates.

3. Organizations that focus on strengths have higher employee engagement.

Reflection Question: What does your hiring track record look like?

Action Step: What will you do to hire the right people to carry on the mission of your organization?

1. Jesus recruited his team of apostles who had no extraordinary skills or education.

2. The twelve apostles were composed of a variety of personalities.

3. Peter, James, and John had access to more events than the other apostles and formed Jesus' inner circle—or management team.

Reflection Question: What qualities do you think Jesus looked for in recruiting his apostles?

Action Step: What will you do differently as you build your team?

CHAPTER 3

Establishing Core Values and Core Purpose

IN THIS CHAPTER, WE COMPARE core values and virtues. Core values provide a behavioral foundation for all members of an organization. Human virtues are firm attitudes, stable dispositions, and habitual perfections of intellect and will that govern our actions, order our passions, and guide our conduct according to faith and reason.

Living the Theological Virtues
You are the light of the world.
A city set on a mountain cannot be hidden.
Nor do they light a lamp and then put it under a bushel basket;
it is set on a lampstand, where it gives light to all in the house.
Just so, your light must shine before others,
that they may see your good deeds and glorify your heavenly Father.
Matthew 5:14-16

Core values are essential and enduring opinions or beliefs of an organization. The real benefit in developing a set of organizational core values is for the individuals inside the organization, and core values are the drivers for behavior. That's why you'll find the core values at the base of the triangle in any strategic plan. Core values provide a behavioral foundation.

As Jesus set the stage for his Church, he was asked, "'Teacher, which commandment in the law is the greatest?' He said to him, 'You shall love the Lord, your God, with all your heart, with all your soul, and with all your mind. This is the greatest and the first commandment. The second is like it: You shall love your neighbor as yourself. The whole law and the prophets depend on these two commandments'" (Matthew 22:36-40)

THEOLOGICAL VIRTUES

If Jesus was participating in a core values meeting today, the following behaviors might have been recorded: *faith, hope, and charity,* In the Catechism of the Catholic Church, faith, hope, and charity are referred to as the theological virtues. Theological virtues come from God.

> The theological virtues are the foundation of Christian moral activity; They are infused by God into the souls of the faithful to make them capable of acting as his children and meriting eternal life.

– Catechism of the Catholic Church 1813

The first theological virtue is *faith.* Faith is belief and commitment to God. Successful entrepreneurs have a belief in their ideas and in the mission of their organizations. *Hope,* the second theological virtue, is trust in God. Successful entrepreneurs trust that the work they do will lead to the success of their mission. The third theological virtue is *charity.* Charity is love. It's the giving of one's time, talent, and treasure for the success of the mission.

Organizations with a foundation of the theological virtues believe in their missions and have hope that their efforts will result in the success of the organizations, and the people involved give freely of their time, talent, and treasure for the success of the mission.

My Experiences with Core Values

I once received a phone call from a client at a large corporation. The company had purchased a manufacturing facility a few years prior and wanted me to work with the president of the facility on a succession program. At the initial meeting with the president, I provided a checklist of common organizational development areas in which businesses typically need help. He indicated his interest in having me help develop a strategic plan. I accepted the assignment and went back to my office to determine how I was going to deliver the program.

The client had built his manufacturing business from scratch. He had purchased the first mold and grown the business over the previous twenty-five years. He had a solid manufacturing background and a strong handle on how to generate profits from the business, but he wanted to learn a formal process of strategic planning to align with his new, much larger parent company.

We began the project by meeting with the management team as a group. Because this particular entrepreneur was very results oriented, I warned him about the first group session. I said, "This first session is going to seem really touchy-feely. I am asking you to trust me, though. We can't skip this part."

I conducted the exercise and asked all the participants to write down the names of five people who, by their behavior only and not their words, demonstrated what was best about the company. I said, "Kevin, who do you have written down on your list?"

He answered, "Amy." I said, "Why did you pick her?" He said, "She is a hard worker and is always willing to take on new responsibilities when asked." Then I said, "Steve, who do you have written down?" He said, "Byron." I said, "Why Byron?" He replied, "Byron is committed."

As we completed the exercise with the entire management team of six people and their lists of five people and their behaviors, some of the same names went up on the board and some common behaviors and themes began to emerge. The team developed the following list of core values for the team:
- Committed
- Hardworking
- Open to growth
- Conscientious

I asked the team, "What happens to people who start to work here and don't exhibit these behaviors?

They answered, "They usually don't stay working here very long, because they don't fit in. If they aren't committed to the position and don't work hard and follow through, they don't fit into the culture."

Then I asked, "If your current boss retired today, and the new boss who was selected was wishy-washy about his or her commitment to the company, put in short days, wasn't interested in learning anything new, and had poor follow-through, how do you think that would work for this team?"

They all agreed that it would be a problem if someone like that replaced the boss, and it would be important for the new boss to demonstrate and "live" the core values they had identified. They also made comments like, "Yeah, that list of core values is really who we are as a company." I could see the team members start to gel a bit with their knowledge of these common bonds.

That training session confirmed for me the importance of establishing core values. It demonstrated that the real value in understanding core values is for the people *inside* the organization. Typically, organizations have three to five core values. When I conduct a core values meeting with a client organization, and we record all the desired behaviors on a flip-chart, themes or key behaviors begin to emerge.

CORE VALUES: DRIVERS FOR BEHAVIOR

Both the core values and the theological virtues communicate to participants in the organization that these are the behaviors, actions, and deeds that will be rewarded. If you want to be happy here, your actions will be in alignment with these values and virtues.

I conducted a core values meeting at a different company last year, and someone came up with the idea of presenting an "employee of the month" award. The company would decide who was most deserving of the award each month based on his or her demonstrating and living the core values of the organization. I thought that was a great idea!

If Jesus was going to give out a disciple of the month award, what would the actions or behaviors be for someone who would be a finalist? Observable actions for faith might be putting God first in all one's decision-making. Hope could be demonstrated by attending daily Mass or seeking the wisdom of the Holy Spirit in prayer to direct all one's actions. Charity could encompass a variety of activities associated with focusing on one's neighbor. I am reminded of the seven corporal works of mercy, including feeding the hungry, giving drink to the thirsty, clothing the naked, sheltering the homeless, caring for the sick, visiting the imprisoned, and burying the dead. Or Jesus might observe us performing the spiritual works of mercy such as counseling the doubtful, instructing the ignorant, admonishing sinners, comforting the afflicted, forgiving offenses, bearing wrongs patiently, and praying for the living and the dead.

CORE VALUES IN BUSINESS

In Michael Gerber's book *Awakening the Entrepreneur Within*, he asks entrepreneurs to identify the reason they are opening their business. He says, "It starts with a longing, an unrequited urge, a feeling, that something is missing in this picture. Something is missing in your life. It starts in you just like it starts in me. This is the time to pursue it. What is your purpose, what is this great business you were called to create?" [xv]

In the early days of my business as I was developing my products and services, I remember working through the exercises in that book to be clear of my core values and purpose. It took me back to the Transfiguration of Jesus. Through his glorification, Jesus provided a hopeful and motivational experience for his followers. I created my business so I could provide hope and motivation to my clients. I decided my first core value for my business would be inspiring. Inspiring is the value of providing hope. The behaviors associated with inspiring others include being enthusiastic, providing encouragement, coaching clients through barriers, and creating an environment in which clients are motivated to succeed. Anyone who works in my business should embody these behaviors and be rewarded for them.

The second core value is results. I like to measure results for my clients. Results are the measurable outcomes clients receive from their investment with our company. It's the scorecard of how our services influence the bottom line for our client organizations. Examples of the results we help our clients achieve are increased sales, efficiency and profitability, lower turnover, and improved efficiency.

Developing Core Values

Core values provide clarity for all levels of an organization. Clearly communicated core values help light the way for leaders of the organization by providing a blueprint for actions and deeds. They help them lead by example. Clearly communicated core values also help all members of the organization to understand what will be valued in the organization. Leaders who are paying attention will look for opportunities to reward behaviors in line with the core values. What gets rewarded gets repeated. What great leaders are really communicating with core values is that these behaviors, actions, and deeds will be rewarded in this organization. If you want to be happy here, your actions will be in alignment with our values.

That's the kind of commitment Jesus expects from his followers. In the Old Testament the Ten Commandments were a promise and a command. In the New Covenant, Jesus writes the law on our hearts. In his Sermon on the Mount he gives us the Beatitudes, blessings, to help us return to a right relationship with God.

Individual Core Values

Because God gave us all a different set of talents, and we are all unique, we will each carry out the theological virtues in a different way. When I teach leadership programs, defining individual core values sits near the top of our agenda. As leaders, if we want to be able to build trust with our people, then our followers need to understand who we are as an individual.

That's why it's important for a leader to be aware of what's important to him or her. In essence, our individual core values will determine our drivers for behavior. If our drivers for behavior are based on our core values, then what we do over time is who we are.

I ask participants to review a list of words and circle the top two that best describe who each of them is as a person. The words are many and varied, including *accountable, family, security, fast pace, competence, competition, passion, leaving a legacy, customer-centric, working under pressure, creative expression*, etc. Each participant shares his or her top two values with the group, and then I ask participants why it's important for them to understand their core values. They typically respond that it will help them gain clarity to find their unique leadership style.

For example, my top two values are credibility and passion. Credibility - actions consistent with words, practicing what one preaches, and walking the walk. Passion - intense emotional excitement, a visible enthusiasm for one's work, an ideal and/or belief. During our discussion, I ask participants, "What do you think would happen if I was a manager, and my employee came into work with a devil-may-care attitude and never followed through when he committed to something?" They usually say, "It probably wouldn't be good for your relationship." I say, "How important do you think it is for my employees to know and understand my core values?"

BUILDING RELATIONSHIPS WITH CORE VALUES

As a sales manager, I remember a particular sales representative who would walk into my office with the weight of the world on his shoulders. He would complain about not being able to figure out how to get a certain account to increase its spending. I responded, "Let's set up a meeting to dig into the situation and build a plan." When the date came for the meeting, the rep showed up half-engaged not seeming to care about the outcome, and not working too hard to collaborate or problem solve. I remember my blood pressure beginning to rise and thinking, "This is your account. If you don't care what happens, why am I spending my time trying to figure this out?" I remember communicating that to the individual that day in a calm manner. It was obvious my "passion" core value was being violated. Similarly, how important is it for me to understand my employee's core values? I know many companies that want to reinforce the importance of core values will make accommodations for employees who choose "family" as a top core value to attend their kids' extracurricular events to honor those core values.

Most of my classroom discussions settle on the importance of building respect for one another and trying to honor the individual's values to build trust and teamwork. For leadership development, being clear on core values helps set the tone for uncovering our leadership voice and being clear on the expectations we have for our followers. Understanding our employees' values centers on building a strong and trusting relationship.

I always suggest that leaders conduct a core values meeting with all team members, either individually or as a group. Some companies I have worked with have conducted the exercise, and each team member taped a copy of his or her top two core values to his or her office window to remind other team members of their values.

In essence, core values are about behaviors. Sometimes I ask participants, "If you retired today, would the people you work with be able to repeat the core values you circled? Would they mention those actions at your retirement party? At your funeral? Would your actions represent the theological virtues of faith, hope, and charity?" It will be our daily actions that determine the answer to that question.

COMMUNICATING CORE VALUES

Jesus said, "You are the light of the world. A city set on a mountain cannot be hidden. Nor do they light a lamp and then put it under a bushel basket; it is set on a lampstand, where it gives light to all in the house. Just so, your light must shine before others, that they may see your good deeds and glorify your heavenly Father" (Matthew 5:14-16). Just as Jesus went high on a mountain-top to deliver his message of the Beatitudes, as leaders we must communicate our organization's core values, as well as our own individual core values.

In Patrick Lencioni's book *The Advantage: Why Organizational Health Trumps Everything Else in Business,*" he provides a diagram to reinforce the importance of organizational health. The first quadrant is *build a cohesive leadership team*, the second quadrant is *create clarity*, the third quadrant is *overcommunicate clarity* and the fourth is *reinforce clarity*. The point Lencioni makes is that when you feel like you have communicated and have beaten something to death in a message, most people are just starting to get what you are trying to say.[xvi] I think the same is true with core values. The lesson here: communicate, communicate, communicate.

> The disciple of Christ must not only keep the faith and live on it, but also profess it, confidently bear witness to it, and spread it:
>
> — *Catechism of the Catholic Church*, 1816

During his three-year mission, Jesus had a rigorous public speaking schedule to communicate his core values and the vision for his Church. As leaders, how can we reinforce the core values in our organizations? I experienced a wonderful example recently while conducting a session from my leadership development program. The leadership team and I were gathered in the boardroom, and as we discussed one of the main objectives in that module — a point about understanding and reinforcing core values to create team unity and higher performance—I asked, "How can we as leaders reinforce the core values in our organization to create unity?" The VP of sales and marketing pointed to the tray ceiling. There, the three main core values were painted on each side of the drop ceiling of the boardroom:

- "The Customer is the Boss - This was intentionally painted on both sides of the ceiling on the shorter ends, so it can be seen from any seat in the room.

- "None of us is as smart as all of us."

- "We will make good products and sell them honestly."

How clever! The same core values are listed on the company website and in marketing materials. This company is obviously making an effort to communicate its core values to employees and customers alike.

CORE PURPOSE

In addition to core values, an organization needs to understand its core purpose. What is an organization's core purpose? Establishing an organization's core purpose answers the question, "Why are we here?" The core purpose is an organization's reason for being. It represents the idealistic motivations for the work and what can be accomplished collectively that can't be done separately. It's what makes a contribution to society; something of value and benefit in establishing a core purpose is to guide, inspire, and not differentiate. Some examples of core purpose statements:

- Walt Disney — To make people happy.

- McDonalds — To be our customers' favorite place and way to eat.

- Amazon — To be earth's most customer centric company; to build a place where people can come to find and discover anything they might want to buy online. [xvii]

An organization's core purpose is unchanging. It's something of which to aspire and is something never fulfilled.

The unchanging core purpose of the Catholic Church is to make disciples of all nations. Through the disciples, Jesus communicated the core purpose for his mission, the Church. He demonstrated the core values of theological virtues from God—faith, hope, and charity—with his actions.

As Jesus delivered consistent communication to his disciples and led by example, he got his disciples to "row in the same direction." In business, highly engaged teams are more likely to achieve their missions when everyone is in alignment with the core values and core purpose of the organization. Establishing core values in organizations provides members of the organization with direction on sought after behaviors. The theological virtues of faith, hope, and charity, along with the corporal and spiritual works for mercy, provide Christians with a framework for living the way God intended.

Chapter Three Highlights

1. Core values are enduring opinions or beliefs of an organization. Clarifying them is beneficial for people inside the organization.

2. Leaders should identify their individual core values.

3. The core purpose of an organization is the reason it exists.

Reflection Question: What are the core values and core purpose of *your* organization?

Action Step: What will you do to live the core values and support the core purpose of your organization?

1. Virtues are similar to core values.

2. The theological virtues of faith, hope, and charity are from God.

3. Jesus preached about the two greatest commandments-- love of God and love of neighbor.

Reflection: Question: In what ways do you live faith, hope and charity?

Action Step: How will you incorporate all three virtues into your daily life?

CHAPTER 4
Developing Key Targets

THIS CHAPTER OUTLINES HOW continuous improvement meetings help businesses identify strategies for leaders and set priorities for the next three to five years. These strategies are called key targets. They are comparable to how Jesus implemented his key targets during his three-year mission.

Jesus Carries His Message
The woman said to him, "Sir, I can see that you are a prophet.
Our ancestors worshiped on this mountain;
but you people say that the place to worship is in Jerusalem.
Jesus said to her, "Believe me, woman, the hour is coming
when you will worship the Father neither on this mountain nor in Jerusalem.
The woman said to him, "I know that the Messiah is coming,
the one called the Anointed; when he comes, he will tell us everything."
Jesus said to her, "I am he, the one who is speaking with you."
John 4:19-21, 25-26

Jesus preached mainly to the Jewish people within a ninety-mile radius, moving frequently from the Sea of Galilee near Capernaum and Bethsaida all the way to Jerusalem near the Dead Sea.

His key target of establishing identity was to speak with authority and demonstrate authority with teaching, healing, and miracles. Jesus demonstrated this authority and acted on his core values and virtues of faith, hope, and charity when he

- Changed the water into wine in Galilee (John 2:1-12).

- Healed a paralyzed man in Capernaum (Matthew 9:1-8, Mark 2:1-12, Luke 5:17-26).

- Calmed a storm on the Sea of Galilee (Matthew 9:23-27, Mark 5:35-41, Luke 8:22-25).

- Fed five thousand people in Bethsaida (Matthew 14:13-21, Mark 6:34-44, Luke 9:10-17, John 6:1-15).

- Walked on the water in the Sea of Galilee (Matthew 14:22-33, Mark 6:45-52, John 6:16-21).

- Raised Lazarus from the dead in Bethany (John 11:1-44).

Another key target for Jesus was to establish his authority as the Son of Man. Jesus was clear on his message, and he used a series of "I AM" statements referenced in the Gospel of John to communicate the message that he was the Messiah. When Jesus spoke, he spoke with authority, indicating he had earned the right to talk about his subject. In the Gospel of John, he said

- "I am the bread of life" (John 6:35).

- "I am the light of the world" (John 8:12).

- "I am the good shepherd" (John 10:11).

- "I am the resurrection and the life" (John 11:25).

Jesus spent a lot of time with his disciples and with large groups of people, but he also blocked time to spend in prayer away from his daily activities of healing and teaching.

My Experience with Key Targets

My first year as a sales representative at the newspaper was a whirlwind. Since I was young and right out of college, I started out in the downtown territory. In addition to meeting my customers, processing their ads, and meeting the daily deadlines of a hectic newspaper, there always seemed to be big projects happening. The first major project in which I participated was the change of an advertising column format going from an eight-column format to a six-column format. As part of this process, every ad had to be changed to fit the new format. That same year, our six-times-a-week newspaper added a Saturday edition. Along with more deadlines came a large promotional campaign. As sales reps, we needed to get our customers interested in running ads on Saturday, too. Then a decision was made to move publication of the newspaper from afternoon to morning delivery. This changed all deadlines again, not to mention half the workforce, including the newsroom and production staff, needed to work an almost entirely different schedule. I remember thinking to myself, "When is this place ever going to settle down?"

Seven years later, when I became a manager and completed a training module on innovation and continuous improvement, I realized this question was best answered by a quote from Alfred North Whitehead: "The art of progress is to preserve order amid change and to preserve change amid order." [xviii] So I kept a copy of that quote taped to my computer screen. It re- minded me that, as a leader in the organization, it was up to me to view my workplace with an attitude of constructive discontent and create change on a regular basis to help us move into the future.

I was fortunate to work for a large professional company started in 1870, composed of multiple divisions. We came together each year in meetings called ACT meetings, held at an off-site location and facilitated by the VP of human resources. We discussed strategic initiatives; conducted SWOT analyses, which identified strengths, weaknesses, opportunities, and threats to the company; and focused on the big picture. It was a good opportunity to work ON the business instead of IN the business.

I always enjoyed those meetings. Many great ideas came from time spent brainstorming outside the office. In organizational language, we call these ideas "key targets." Eventually, a lot of the ideas ended up as formal projects on somebody's "to do" list for the year. We called them organizational objectives or projects, and typically managers had to plan for all the resources needed to complete the projects and develop plans for implementation within a specified time frame. Unlike core values and purpose, which are unchanging, key targets are ever changing and help organizations move forward. Even if an organization is one hundred years old or more, the people who lead it still have to look for creative ways to achieve its core purpose and build for the future.

Since my area of responsibility was generating sales, my key targets included the creation of new products like niche publications, implementation of sales training, and introduction of consultative selling tools that utilized research and retail purchasing trends. We helped our advertising clients by adjusting rates and solving pricing problems while implementing new technologies and digital processes, which streamlined production.

One of the main areas in which I see new managers struggle is in budgeting time to complete key targets. Many new managers have not learned how to dedicate some time in their day for planning, developing relationships, gathering data on problem areas of their business, and assessing performance issues. In other words, they don't spend enough time working on things that are important but not urgent. As a result, the important key targets assigned to them for implementation often fall short or are left completely undone. When asked, "Why not?" most managers would respond, "Because I was too busy."

KEY TARGETS FOR JESUS

If Jesus had a list of key targets for his three-year mission, it might have included the following areas:

- Establish authority as Son of Man.

- Preach the Gospel in a ninety-mile radius of Jerusalem.

- Gain disciples through teaching, healing and miracles.

Since key targets often involve a strategy, determining how and where to market a new idea or venture is critical. A former executive I worked with described organizations that didn't have a really good strategy for market growth as "trying to boil the ocean."

IMPLEMENTING KEY TARGETS

Implementing key targets is a huge stumbling block for many leaders. This group typically deals with all the responsibilities of direct reports, including hiring, firing, training, and coaching. Managing people takes time. People are a huge drain on a manager's time. In addition, these same managers are saddled with planning, organizing, and delegating the details of key targets or various other department projects. It has been my experience that many companies offer little training in these critical areas of development for new and existing managers. I'm quite sure that if I had not received help in these areas early in my management career, I would not have successfully achieved the goals that were my responsibility as a new manager.

When I was a new manager, it was difficult to have open sales positions, which required recruiting experienced sales representatives to manage the difficult requirements, while another two or three sales reps constantly needed my time for questions, and another rep was barely making it. Simultaneously, I managed problems associated with production and other departments. When was there time to implement new products and kick off seemingly massive key targets handed down from the top as important? Until I learned the necessary tools to help me gain control of that situation, I had huge stacks of folders with projects going nowhere. I was reactive and overwhelmed in my position, and I felt excessively busy, frazzled, and like a total failure. That's why I developed my leadership program. During the program we address the critical skills managers need to plan and implement key targets and help lead the organization forward.

TIME MANAGEMENT

One of the first methods we discuss in this program is time. Participants complete an assessment to gauge their skill levels in the areas of attitude, goal and priority setting, analyzing time, planning, scheduling, interruptions, meetings, written communications, delegation, procrastination, and team time. After evaluating themselves, participants complete a time log for a normal week and see how much time they are spending in each of Charles Hummel's four quadrants known as the Tyranny of the Urgent.

TYRANNY OF THE URGENT

	Urgent	Not Urgent
Important	**I** Deadlines Crises Urgent Problems Firefighting	**II** Planning Prevention Initiatives Relationship Building Staff Development Developing New Opportunities
Not Important	**III** Interruptions Some Phone Calls Some Reports Some Paperwork	**IV** Time Wasters Solitaire Unfocused Social Media Internet Surfing with no Purpose

Original concept by Charles E. Hummel.

The first quadrant is the urgent and important quadrant, where many new leaders spend most of their time. This is the quadrant I refer to as "firefighting" - everything is important, and you have to deal with everything now! The second quadrant is the important but not urgent quadrant. This is where I aim to get participants to spend more time, because time spent in this quadrant usually improves overall performance in the leader's role. Important but not urgent activities include planning important projects that represent key targets for the organization, setting up meetings to move those projects forward, meeting with staff members to track their progress toward goal achievement, building relationships, and focusing on preventative measures to prevent problems. The third quadrant is based on time spent on things that are urgent but not important. This might entail activities a leader perceives as interruptions or important to others. The fourth quadrant is not important and not urgent. This would include things like surfing the Internet with no real purpose or playing games. Typically, I don't see conscientious leaders spending much time in this quadrant. [xix]

Once leaders have an honest picture of how they are spending their time, they usually find they are not spending much time on completing key targets. They begin to understand it will be imperative to "block in" or schedule time in their weekly schedules to plan, prioritize, and implement long-term projects.

I have seen firsthand that when a leader begins to shift time allocation to more time spent in the important but not urgent quadrant, his or her ability to become proactive versus reactive is significant. When leaders start to actively schedule meetings to address difficult, long-standing problems in organizations, begin to engage their staffs to solve problems, and then break the solutions down into manageable steps with plans and follow through on those plans, the impact is huge. It is a game changer!

IMPLEMENTING CHANGE

Another game changing method for leaders is implementing change. This process begins with having a continuous improvement mindset and identifying areas of an organization that are not performing well or wanting to take an area of the organization to the next level. Best practices in this area show participants how to analyze problems, gather facts associated with the problems, and then brainstorm problem statements in a positive and safe environment. Learning to facilitate a meeting like this and then consistently engaging staff participation are important tools for every leader who must determine how to implement a key target.

We used this tool recently with my local Rotary club in order to increase engagement of club members. The entire membership of more than 150 was invited to participate in an improvement meeting on a Saturday morning. It was set up as a meeting that could take the organization to the next level. About a dozen loyal Rotary club members participated in the meeting. We first identified membership as an area in which we wanted to improve. After analyzing the problem (opportunity for improvement) further, we decided to focus on engagement of club members instead of membership.

Charles Kettering, an American inventor, said, "A problem well stated is a problem half-solved."[xx] We brainstormed how we could increase engagement of Rotary club members and had dozens of ideas. Once recorded, we prioritized the ideas and highlighted those we wanted to focus on for implementation. A big idea that came from the club president was the goal of having at least 50 percent of members as participants in the Paul Harris Fellowship program. The Paul Harris Fellow recognition acknowledges individuals who contribute, or who have contributions made in their names, of one thousand dollars to The Rotary Foundation of Rotary International. It was established in 1957 to show appreciation for and to encourage substantial contributions to what was then the foundation's only program, Rotary Foundation Fellowships for Advanced Study, the precursor to ambassadorial scholarships. As a result of clarifying that goal at the meeting and then sharing the goal with the entire membership, the number of Paul Harris Fellow participants went from 41 percent of club members to 55 percent of total club members. Rotary club financial giving in the Paul Harris Fellowship program grew by 35 percent. My local Rotary club now has one of the largest numbers of participants in the program in the state. This same kind of improvement meeting can be held on most any topic on which you want to see an improvement or take the organization to the next level. I like this story, especially since it involves a nonprofit organization. In a volunteer organization, you can't make anyone do anything. In volunteer organizations, everything is volunteer, and as a result, you must use tools and methods for engagement and participation to gain cooperation and get results.

PLANNING

In addition to understanding the steps of conducting an improvement meeting, planning is vital for success. If leaders conduct positive and successful meetings with their staffs and stakeholders, there will typically be many ideas for implementation. And once the best ideas are selected, it's time to implement them. This can be a difficult task for any leader who doesn't know how to plan. How do you eat an elephant? One bite at a time.

I recently coached a leader who had a series of projects handed down to her from strategic planning meetings held by the corporate leaders in the organization. She was just returning from maternity leave and was overwhelmed with the number of projects she needed to implement in addition to her current workload as a supervisor. As part of my leadership program, she had six personalized coaching sessions with me. My role as her coach was to help her to achieve the goals she set for herself during the time period of the program. When she came to her meetings, we reviewed her goal sheet, and I asked what she wanted to work on that day. She identified a major training project she was responsible for implementing. First, I asked her to write a vision for the project. I then asked her to think of everything that came to her mind in order to achieve this goal. I had her write each activity on a sticky note. Once she had about twenty sticky notes, we began to organize them by category. We sorted them into four groups—curriculum, technology, communication, and follow-up—and then took out a planning worksheet and assigned every sticky note an action step. She looked at the calendar and set a due date for each action step. Next, she determined who else, if anyone, could help her with that step, and recorded his or her name in the blank.

Finally, she visualized what she wanted as a result of completing that action step and recoded it in the blank titled "expected outcome." During our one- hour meeting, she transferred all the sticky notes with due dates, people responsible, and expected outcomes. She was able to complete a plan for the entire project over a six-month time frame. She left the meeting focused and confident that she had built a step-by-step plan to achieve her project. When she came back for another meeting a few weeks later, we did the same thing for another major project she was responsible for. She said to me, "This really works." I loved it!

DELEGATION

Since time is such a major barrier in implementing key targets, I usually ask, "What process are you using for delegation?" It doesn't matter if I am working with a brand new manager or a seasoned business owner; I usually get the same look—a blank stare. Applying a successful method for delegation is probably the biggest game changer for most leaders. The inability to delegate has even been attributed to presidents of the United States. If a leader cannot master this method, it will probably prevent a successful transition in most organizations.

I usually start the group portion of any session with a success story. One day, I started the session by asking, "Who would be willing to share a success story?" The leader of one of the product divisions said, "I will."

I was pleased that he had volunteered, since we had spent his last individual coaching meeting working on a delegation plan to transfer some of the customer service work he was performing to an experienced customer service person. He explained to the group that he had developed a vision for the result of the work and what it would look like when the customer service was being performed by someone else. He explained to the group why he had selected that person and the attributes and strengths she had that would make her successful. Finally, he reviewed how he conducted a delegation meeting with the recipient and asked her to develop a plan. He said the meeting went well, and he was confident she would do a great job. I asked him, "What did you do differently?" At first he didn't really get what I was asking him. I asked him again, "What did you have to do differently to accomplish this delegation project?"

He responded very bluntly, "I quit being such a control freak!" Oh, my gosh, I couldn't believe the honesty. It was refreshing. I thought it was totally awesome and a huge breakthrough for him and for his company. It has been my observation that, in addition to letting go of the work psychologically, using a specific form, writing down the expected results, and communicating with the delegation recipient throughout the process lead to consistent success. When leaders consistently use a process for delegation and follow-up, they are finally able to accomplish key targets for their organizations.

Summary

Organizations evolve. Core values and purpose remain the same, just like the theological virtues that come from God—faith, hope, and charity. Key targets are ever changing. They are big projects that keep organizations viable in the marketplace. Just like prayer is done off-line from the hustle bustle of our daily lives, key targets are strategies that are developed off-site when leaders have a chance to analyze and think ahead to the future. It may take organizations three to five years to implement these strategies when they are drilled down into projects. These projects need to be communicated by someone who has earned the right to deliver the message and have a well-defined plan in place and a call to action for all involved.

Jesus blocked out time for prayer. He kept the vision of his mission at the forefront of his mind and carried out the key targets of establishing his identity and authority from God with the Jewish people in a defined region.

CHAPTER FOUR HIGHLIGHT

1. Conducting continuous improvement meetings helps organizations identify key targets - three to five year areas of focus and projects.

2. Implementing key targets is challenging for many leaders and requires time management skills

3. Planning and delegation are tools for executing key targets.

Reflection Question: Which key targets are you responsible for implementing in your organization?

Action Step: How will you use the concepts of time management, implementing change, and planning and delegation to accomplish the key targets in your organization?

1. Jesus carried his message to the Jews in a ninety-mile radius of his hometown of Nazareth.

2. One of Jesus' key targets was to demonstrate his authority as the Son of God. He accomplished this by using a series of "I AM" statements along with his teaching, healing, and miracles.

3. Jesus blocked out time for prayer.

Reflection Question: What lessons have you learned from Jesus about implementing key targets in your daily life?

Action Step: What do you need to block time for in your faith life?

CHAPTER 5
Measuring Progress

THIS CHAPTER DISCUSSES HOW ORGANIZATIONS measure performance and the processes available for implementation as compared to how Jesus and the Church would evaluate the success of a mission.

Conversions of the Heart
Then he summoned his twelve disciples
and gave them authority over unclean spirits
to drive them out
and to cure every disease and every illness.
Matthew 10:1

Jesus was clear in his instructions to his disciples:

Jesus sent out these Twelve after instructing them thus, "Do not go into pagan territory or enter a Samaritan town. Go rather to the lost sheep of the house of Israel. As you go, make this proclamation: 'The kingdom of heaven is at hand.' Cure the sick, raise the dead, cleanse lepers, drive out demons. Without cost you have received; without cost you are to give. Do not take gold or silver or copper for your belts; no sack for the journey, or a second tunic, or sandals, or walking stick. The laborer deserves his keep. Whatever town or village you enter, look for a worthy person in it, and stay there until you leave. As you enter a house, wish it peace. If the house is worthy, let your peace come upon it; if not, let your peace return to you. Whoever will not receive you or listen to your words - go outside that house or town and shake the dust from your feet."

— Matthew 10:5-14

Jesus gave his disciples the specific activities he wanted them to take action on. His disciples followed his instructions. They did this so that people would repent of their sins and believe in the kingdom of God.

ACTIVITIES VERSUS RESULTS

When I begin teaching the module on improving performance in my leadership program, I always start with the question "What's the difference between activities and results?" I usually get something like, "Results are what we get from performing activities." I heard it best from one of my clients a few months back. He said he was a swimmer as a child. One day, he was at swim practice, and his coach was watching him paddle like crazy. During that time, my client never lifted up his head. When he finally popped his head out of the water, he was a long way from his desired destination. His coach said to him, "Did you realize you have been swimming in circles?" He was so focused on the activity of paddling hard that he took his eyes off his destination. Despite his hard work, he did not achieve his result. Had he paddled hard *and* taken the time to lift his head occasionally, he would have been much closer. It was a great story to demonstrate the difference between focusing on activities and results. Succession management requires a focus on both activities and results.

Measuring Individual Performance

I learned this the hard way. In my first role as a manager at twenty-nine years old, I went from having zero to nine direct reports. Prior to my promotion, I was managing the sales territory with the most revenue. It was extremely difficult to extricate myself from performing the activities in the territory and transfer the strong relationships I had built with my customers. Six months into my management role, I was still doing the same activities that had made me a successful sales rep.

The problem was that I wasn't getting the results I wanted as a manager. It took my participation in a development program for me to clarify the activities I needed to add to my schedule and delegate out of my schedule to become successful. I needed to stop doing sales activities like picking up and processing ads and performing service work for specific accounts and start adding leadership activities like setting goals, building relationships with direct reports, meeting with them to help develop strategies to achieve their goals, and working with the production department on preventative measures to reduce errors. I also had a big aha moment when I had to write down the results of the entire team. I realized the only way to hit my goal was by making sure everyone in the department hit their goals.

Indeed, I needed to make a drastic change in how I approached my work. Once I had that clarity, there was no stopping me. I was able to implement the activities that would help me be successful. That's why it's so critical for managers to spend time understanding their roles as leaders and what they are expected to achieve by developing a list of intended results and the corresponding activities to help them get there.

Defining Roles and Responsibilities

Participants in my leadership program are asked to write down the reason their jobs exist. This helps them understand the bigger picture of how their roles fit into the organization and its goals. All participants get a whole pack of sticky notes as part of their program materials. Participants write down all the activities they perform in their roles. They write down things they know they should be doing, too, even if they aren't doing the activity currently. For example, when I first started as a manager, I knew I should be providing sales training to my direct reports, but my ability to actually implement that complex activity was way out of my skill set at that point. By writing things down, I could aspire to implement them, even if not right away.

JOB RESULT CATEGORIES

Next, we organize the sticky notes into results categories. Typical category titles for a group of sticky notes for a sales manager position are *Sales, Production,* and *Customer Service.* Production manager categories might be *Production-Throughput, Safety, Quality,* and *Inventory.* Other positions might include categories like *Compliance, Purchasing, Scheduling, Financial Reporting* and *IT.* Every manager with direct reports puts all the sticky notes related to hiring, training, and firing into the category called *Staffing.*

INDIVIDUAL ACCOUNTABILITY

Once every sticky note has been arranged into a category, we establish a performance standard or desired measurement for each category. This is where the rubber meets the road in this whole process. Each group of sticky notes needs a measurement to gauge whether progress is being made in that category. I ask the participants to make them SMART: that is, specific, measurable, attainable, results-oriented and time-phased. "Doran's original definition tied in five criteria: specific, measurable, assignable, realistic, and time-related."[xxi]

Examples of performance standards:

• Returns are less than 5% of annual revenue by 12/31/20XX.

• Inventory does not exceed $15,000 each month.

• Sales from new clients increase by 20% by 12/31/20XX.

Often, many of the result categories participants have are not currently being measured. I then ask what the current data reveals to them: "What is the percentage of returns to annual revenue now? What's a realistic number that represents growth?" I also make sure they are setting standards within their span of control. It's unrealistic to set a standard for an area that you cannot control. When the exercise is completed, it contains the reason the leader's position exists in the organization, the result categories for the position, the activities that will need to be performed, and the desired performance standards for each category. The leader has a document that serves as a blueprint for his or her top performance in the role.

ORGANIZATIONAL ACCOUNTABILITY

Organizations use the same process to keep track of their progress. Bain Management's Tools and Trends survey indicates that these same management principles are used today with tools known as customer relationship management (CRM), benchmarking, employee engagement surveys, strategic planning, and balanced scorecards.[xxii] These management tools have a few things in common. First, they help leaders keep track of progress and measure important performance indicators in an organization. Second, the clarity the information brings helps to get everyone in the organization rowing in the same direction, or as I, a longtime choir member and director, like to say, "Get everyone singing from the same hymnal."

THE COMPLEXITY OF EXECUTION

One of the biggest reasons becoming a new leader is so complex is that the role changes. New leaders move from being responsible for their own set of activities and results to understanding the organizational activities and results of every person who reports to them. In this new role, not only are leaders responsible for understanding the activities and expected results for each position in their area of responsibility, but they also need to be able to see and communicate how all the jobs tie into the big picture of the organization.

For example, how does the position of a maintenance worker who cleans floors tie into the success of a multi-million-dollar car company? If leaders don't have clarity on the roles in their area of responsibility and are not able to communicate clearly about how these jobs tie into the success of the organization with the people performing these roles, there will likely be a high level of disengagement among the people in this department.

Measurement Brings Accountability

I recently read an online article criticizing the use of organizational measuring tools. The author of the article noted that the whole concept was outdated and that many organizations are measuring the wrong things. While I believe in some cases companies are not measuring the right areas, abandoning this method would be akin to throwing out the baby with the bathwater. There is no doubt this process makes participants uncomfortable. The use of performance standards ushers in a level of accountability for results that many will not accept. This is the hardest of all the concepts I deliver as a trainer and coach, but once mastered, it is probably the most important in terms of seeing real changes in performance.

Succession management requires that leaders in organizations understand the importance of performance standards in key areas of their organizations. In addition, a main part of their job is to measure the progress toward these performance standards and communicate how things are going on a regular basis.

Measuring Organizational Progress-The Church

How is the Church that Jesus started progressing? According to the Center for Applied Research in the Apostolate (CARA), in 2014, there were 1.229 billion Catholics in the world. From 1970 to 2014, the world's population of Catholics increased by 576 million. In 2014, there were 16.4 million baptisms, 2.7 million Catholic weddings, 10.5 million first communions, and 8.5 million confirmations worldwide in the Catholic Church.[xxiii] Certainly these performance indicators are very impressive.

Engagement as a Key Performance Indicator

How could the application of SMART tools give Catholics a better way to measure their progress? Matthew Kelly has found some startling statistics about engaged Catholics versus reported Catholics. Although there were 66.6 million registered Catholics in the United States in 2014, most of them were not fully engaged. What is fully engaged?

Matthew Kelly studied the concept of dynamic Catholics in his book, *The Four Signs of a Dynamic Catholic*. According to the Dynamic Catholic Institute, the Pareto principle, or the 80/20 rule, didn't hold up in terms of engaged Catholics. The research revealed that 6.4 percent of registered parishioners contribute 80 percent of the volunteer hours in a parish, and 6.8 percent of registered parishioners make 80 percent of the financial contributions. And there is an 84 percent overlap between the two groups. Kelly refers to highly engaged parishioners as "the seven percent."[xxiv]

What does a fully engaged Catholic look like? Kelly's research in his book *The Four Signs of a Dynamic Catholic* underscores four signs:

1. **Prayer** - Dynamic Catholics have a *daily* commitment to prayer. They have a structured way of praying and many pray at the same time daily.

2. **Study** - Dynamic Catholics spend on average 14 minutes each day learning more about the faith.

3. **Generosity** - The seven percent are universally described as being generous, not just with money and time, but with their love, appreciation, praise, virtue, and encouragement.

4. **Evangelization** - Having seen how a vibrant spiritual life has transformed them and every aspect of their lives, highly engaged Catholics want others to experience the joy that flows from having a dynamic relationship with God. [xxv]

If I were helping someone design a document to measure his or her progress as a Catholic, these four categories would contain great activities to measure. A Catholic could set up activities for each area that might include reading books, committing prayer time, implementing charitable giving, or talking with people about his or her faith. I recently attended a Bible study program on the Book of James. During one of the small group exercises, my group members and I were talking about the Rosary. As we discussed prayer and the opportunity for graces available by saying the Rosary, one lady was very adamant about the need to say it every day. She said with all sincerity and authority, "Our Lady of Fatima said, 'Pray the Rosary daily.' We need to say it every day!" I found myself resenting her comments. Where would I find the time to commit to saying the Rosary every day? "That's a little over the top, isn't it?" I thought. I did, however, respect this woman. She was very knowledgeable in all areas of Bible study. After that meeting, I decided to take her advice and started to pray the Rosary daily.

The most amazing thing about the Rosary is that Mary made fifteen promises to those who recite it daily. These promises of Mary show us how the Rosary serves as a spiritual weapon that every soldier for Christ and his Church needs to fight successfully in the spiritual battle that makes up much of our earthly sojourn. Clearly praying the Rosary is a beneficial activity. It would seem that saying the Rosary is one indication of being a dynamic Catholic. But what is the performance standard for being a dynamic Catholic? What is the result of our generosity prayer, study, and evangelization?

The Rigor of Measurement

New leaders learn to make adjustments and plan future changes based on the information they get from monitoring the performance of their direct reports and from financial reporting. I recently hired that lady I met in my Bible study class to help me with my financial reporting. Each month, she enters all the invoices and receipts from my business into QuickBooks. At the end of each month, she reconciles the information from my receipts and bank statements to make sure they are matching. Once she has reconciled the information, she delivers a set of accurate financial reports to me so that I can measure the success of the business and determine what kind of changes we need to make to keep the business on course.

Just like leaders make adjustments in their organizations from the information in a financial statement, Christians make adjustments in their lives based on the information from their examination of conscience. In an examination of conscience, we review our activities from a past time period and determine how they have affected our relationship with God. Once we have done a thorough analysis, we determine adjustments we need to make to reconcile our relationship with him.

An examination of conscience will help us make adjustments along the way. Here are some sample questions to ask yourself at the end of the day:

- How did I use my time today?

- What good did I do for others today?

- Have I been honest in my business dealings?

- Did I hurt anyone? Did I gossip about others?

- How can I overcome my obstacles?

Remember to always thank the Lord for the good in your life as well as the challenging times that make us stronger. Ultimately, our eternal life is in the kingdom of God. Heaven is where the rubber meets the road. The activities that we perform lead to a conversion of heart. Only Jesus can see into our hearts and reward us with eternal life in the kingdom of God.

SUCCESS OF THE MISSION

Correspondingly, I think Jesus would measure the success of the Church based on the total number of "conversions of the heart."

> "Jesus calls to conversion. This call is an essential part of the proclamation of the kingdom:…It is by faith in the Gospel and by Baptism that one renounces evil and gains salvation, that is, the forgiveness of all sins and the gift of new life."

> — *Catechism of the Catholic Church, 1427*

While Catholics have a lot of key performance indicators to help them on their path, it seems as though measuring our individual progress toward actual results is an inside job. We can imitate high performers with great habits and block in the appropriate activities of prayer, study, generosity, and evangelization. But only Jesus can see what's in our hearts and give us our final evaluations in the end.

Succession management requires leaders to monitor the activities and results of each individual while measuring and communicating the combined organizational results. This provides the necessary structure and blueprint for a high performing organization to transition into the future.

CHAPTER FIVE HIGHLIGHTS

1. The use of measurement tools as a guide for performance is still prevalent today.

2. New leaders need to understand their roles, why their jobs exist, activities necessary for success, and a performance standard for each area of their responsibility.

3. Performance standards should be SMART (specific, measurable, attainable, results-oriented, and time-phased).

Reflection Question: What kind of tools are you using to measure progress in your organization?

Action Step: What system will you use to track performance individually and organizationally?

1. Catholics represent 17 percent of the world's population.

2. Dynamic Catholics incorporate prayer, study, generosity and evangelization into their daily lives.

3. A regular examination of conscience guides us in our right relationship with God, which will be evaluated by Jesus at our time of death.

Reflection Question: How engaged are you in your faith?

Action Step: What will you do to maintain your relationship with Jesus?

CHAPTER 6
Selecting a New CEO

JESUS HANDED PETER THE KEYS to the kingdom. This chapter discusses best practices for selecting the next CEO and how we can learn from Jesus and his selection process.

Jesus Hands Peter the Keys to the Kingdom
Simon Peter said in reply,
"You are the Messiah, the Son of the living God."
Jesus said to him in reply, "Blessed are you, Simon son of Jonah.
For flesh and blood has not revealed this to you,
but my heavenly Father. And so I say to you,
you are Peter, and upon this rock I will build my church,
and the gates of the netherworld shall not prevail against it."
Matthew 16:16-18

I work with business owners and executives in the area of succession management. Recently, I had a business owner who was interested in learning more about what it would take to have a plan in place to transition his business into the future. It was a family business, and one of the owners was contemplating retiring within the next few years. There was a mix of family and non-family members on his management team. After we discussed the importance of having a strategic plan in place, we talked about who might succeed him in the CEO role. Based on my client's needs, I knew that an assessment tool of some sort was one of the solutions I was planning to propose for his succession plan. I made the recommendation for my client to complete a talent audit.

Talent Audits

A talent audit is the process of having the owner and each member of the management team complete a comprehensive assessment. The owner had been successful in his position for many years, so we used his assessment to build a performance model for the CEO role at his company. We also used a job analysis survey to dig deeper into the skills necessary to succeed in the role as a top performer. Finally, we looked in the O*Net database for positions that were similar to this CEO. "The O*NET program is the nation's primary source of occupational information. Central to the project is the O*NET database, containing information on hundreds of standardized and occupation-specific descriptors."[xxvi] We used this database as a resource to build a performance model for a CEO in the transportation industry.

My client, the CEO, agreed to complete the talent audit and we assessed him and his five management team members. Once the assessments were complete, which took each person about one hour, we had the data needed to run a report for each person on the management team. The reports compared each team member to the prepared performance model. As outlined in chapter two of this book, each management team member was given an overall percentage match in addition to a percentage match for the cognitive, behavioral, and interest areas for the transportation CEO position. I think the scores ranged from an overall high match of 86 percent to low match in the 50 percent range. Finally, we ran a candidate matching report that summarized the percentage match of all candidates for the position in descending order. This process gave the CEO factual data with which to make some very important decisions. Since the CEO saw his assessment information, he was able to gain self-awareness and pinpoint the specific skills and behaviors that had led him to success and also identify areas in which he was not as successful.

Since then, I have used this same process for many management teams. In all cases, the CEOs were grateful for the information about themselves, as well as the information about their management team.

Management Team Audits for Team Building

I have also conducted management team audits with the goal not succession, but rather focused on team building. These audits include each person on the management team (including the CEO) completing an assessment and receiving an individual report with his or her results, which helps the team members to better understand themselves. We also run a team report to help each member of the team see how he or she is different from the others. I have advised CEOs to use the information to coach their management team to higher levels of performance, based on the coaching reports generated for each person.

Not only does the team audit process provide the CEO with the necessary "job fit" information to make the best hiring decision, but it also provides information on how the team can work together better. The management team audit is based on the famous Michael Jordan quote "Talent wins games, but teamwork and intelligence wins championships."[xxvii] A good succession plan will not just be about filling the CEO position with the right person. A great succession plan identifies all the critical positions in an organization and builds a top performer model for all positions, so there is a team in place with capable people to keep things moving into the future.

Entrepreneurs versus CEOs

I have also noticed there is a difference in the performance patterns among CEOs (chief executive officers) and business owners (entrepreneurs). It is common to see a reasonably high learning index on both patterns, but there is a noticeable difference in the behavior of an entrepreneur versus an executive.

Entrepreneur behaviors seem to be extreme. Consequently, they seem to have more scores that reveal their behaviors to be extreme. Chief executive officers differ a little from these extremes. Marshall Goldsmith hints at this theory in his book *What Got You Here Won't Get You There: How Successful People Become Even More Successful.* He makes the point that the behaviors that propel people to positions of leadership may not be valued when they attain higher level leadership positions. He highlights the importance of behaviors and relationships as you climb the corporate ladder [xxviii] That's why I think the CEO patterns I have observed are slightly less extreme than those of entrepreneurs. Corporate settings require more collaboration, and there are more relationships to manage in a potentially political environment. I have seen this firsthand when a small business owner sells his company to a corporation and stays on as the president. It can be very difficult to have extreme behaviors. The same traits and characteristics that were critical factors in building a successful business from scratch may not be valued as an entrepreneur moves into a corporate environment. Extreme behaviors are not always appreciated or valued in some corporate environments, and entrepreneurs with extreme scores outside their new CEO performance models have to learn how to adapt their behaviors and conform to the needs of the position.

This is just my observation and hypothesis. The best practice in any case is to assess a top performer for critical positions in the organization and build a performance model to evaluate candidates.

Jesus Hands Peter the Keys to the Kingdom

If Jesus had conducted a talent audit, who do you suppose he would have assessed? He would probably have assessed the three people in his inner circle Peter, James, and John. As we outlined in chapter two, Peter was quick to speak and the most extreme of the Twelve, with his impulsive nature. Peter became the rock, a fearless missionary for the Church. That's pretty similar to an entrepreneur's pattern with high energy and assertiveness scores. Impulsive and emotional, Peter spoke before he thought many times. Rash in word and act alike, he was full of zeal and enthusiasm. Peter would probably have scored low in objective judgment, which means he was emotional. Peter was the first to get out of the boat and follow Jesus when he walked on the water. I bet

Peter would have scored high in decisiveness, as a lot of entrepreneurs do. He is also the apostle who struck the high priest's servant, cutting off his ear as Jesus was being arrested. Again, a low objective judgment score is where a portion of the emotional drive comes from, but it can also cause one to lose perspective. Peter quickly emerged as a leader among the disciples. Extreme scores in a behavioral assessment are pretty consistent with the entrepreneurial performance patterns based on my experience. Starting any new venture is an extremely challenging situation, and extreme behaviors can be an asset.

James could be intense, with periods of anger and rage. I'm thinking James was more skeptical and would have scored low on outlook. John, the disciple that Jesus loved, was especially loyal to Jesus. I bet he would have scored high on accommodation. He is credited with writing five books in the New Testament. In order to write that many books, he must not have found it difficult to be alone, which leads me to believe he would have scored on the lower side of sociability.

I often use the phrase from the Tom Rath and Barry Conchie book, *Strengths Based Leadership: Great Leaders, Teams, and Why People Follow* "Although individuals need not be well-rounded, teams should be." [xxix] Jesus built a diverse team of apostles with complementary behavioral traits to spread his Gospel message.

From his trusted inner circle, Jesus chose one man to lead the Church. What process did he use? We might find some similarities between his approach and the three-legged stool approach to selecting future leaders.

THREE-LEGGED STOOL APPROACH

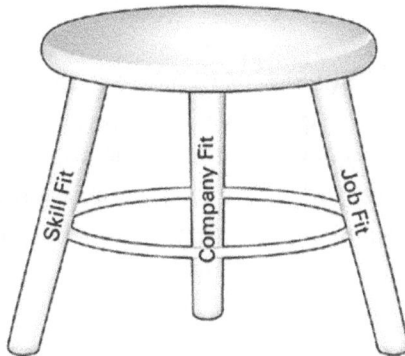

SKILL FIT: THE RESUME

Skill fit is defined as information about a potential candidate's work history and skills. This is usually found on the candidate's resume. It is based upon education, training, and experience. Where did the candidate get his or her education? What did he or she study? What are his or her training experiences, and what has he or she accomplished in different work experiences? Does the candidate have the commensurate skills for the position? This is just the ticket to get into the game.

COMPANY FIT: THE INTERVIEW

The second leg of the stool is company fit. Company fit is the likelihood that a job candidate will be able to conform and adapt to the core values of an organization. Does the candidate share the same values? Does the company even have a set of core values to match the candidate up against? Many don't. Company fit identifies how a candidate for a position will fit into the culture of the organization based on his or her attitudes, values, demeanor, appearance, and integrity. In order to measure how someone will fit into an organization, we need to go back to chapter three where we cover core values and core purpose. If a company has not documented or clarified this information, it will be hard to make good decisions in this area. If an organization has identified its core values and core purpose, it will be easier to ask applicant questions in this area. What is your first impression of the candidate? Is he or she dressed professionally, if that is a requirement of the position? Good interviewers ask questions to get the applicant to talk about specific experiences from other jobs and really listen to understand if he or she will fit into the culture of the organization.

JOB FIT: THE ASSESSMENT

As we discussed in chapter two, an assessment tool is invaluable in measuring job fit. It provides consistent, in-depth, and objective insight into an individual's thinking and reasoning style, relevant behavioral traits, and occupational interests and matches them to specific jobs in an organization. By following the three-legged stool approach and using assessments as one-third of the decision making process, organizations reduce the risk of making a bad hire, which could cost the organization time and money.

Did Peter have skill fit? Over the three-year period of his ministry, Jesus preached mainly within a ninety-mile radius. Peter had the on-the-job training as he accompanied Jesus when he spoke in the temple and in the countryside. Peter was with Jesus when he fed the crowd of five thousand and attended festivals with him. Peter was in the boat when Jesus calmed a storm on the Sea of Galilee. Peter was one of only three disciples allowed to witness the raising of the daughter of Jairus, the Transfiguration, and invited to pray with Jesus in the Garden of Gethsemane. Peter was the audacious disciple who got out of the boat on the Sea of Galilee to walk on the water toward Jesus. Peter had real world mission experience based on the fact that he participated in the mission of the Twelve. Peter must have acquired the appropriate work history needed to achieve the skill fit to succeed in the position.

What about company fit? "Simon Peter said in reply, 'You are the Messiah, the Son of the living God.' Jesus said to him in reply, 'Blessed are you, Simon son of Jonah. For flesh and blood has not revealed this to you, but my heavenly Father. And so I say to you, you are Peter, and upon this rock I will build my church, and the gates of the netherworld shall not prevail against it'" (Matthew 16:16-18). Peter was given information that the rest of the inner circle didn't have, and as a result, he was the first leader of the Church.

Based on the book, *Good To Great*, we know that "ten out of eleven good-to-great CEOs came from inside the company." [xxx] This means that a high percentage of managers in any organization will be promoted from within. If the internal candidate has demonstrated him or herself to be a good match for the culture in the past, he or she should maintain that match in the future. In addition, a good match in the area of company fit should demonstrate an understanding of everything we have discussed in the previous chapters of this book. A top candidate should live the core values and lead based on the core purpose. He or she should have a track record of implementing key targets and have successfully transitioned to new roles throughout his or her career in the organization. He or she should have a strong understanding of how the organization measures progress and understand the desired results for all departments in the organization.

Just as Peter "got it" he understood the mission of the Church and that Jesus was the Son of God - a top candidate "gets" and believes in the mission of the organization.

Finally, what about job fit? Jesus must have believed that Peter would be able to handle the mental demands of the position, be comfortable with the environment and people in this role, and have an interest in leading the Church as first pope.

COMMITMENT

In addition to skill fit, company fit, and job fit, Peter was committed to the mission of the Church; just as a top candidate should be committed to the mission of an organization. Elise Harris from the Catholic News Agency quotes Pope Francis in his homily on June 30, 2014, in Vatican City: "Pope Francis focused his homily for the feast of the First Roman Martyrs on the witness of martyrdom, and prayed for all who continue to be persecuted for their faith, particularly in the Middle East. 'The Church grows thanks to the blood of the martyrs. This is the beauty of martyrdom It begins with witness... day after day, and it can end like Jesus, the first martyr, the first witness, the faithful witness: with blood.'" [xxxi] Not only was Peter the definitive witness for the Church, he was martyred.

In most companies and organizations, that level of commitment translates into sacrifice. In addition to meeting all the criteria mentioned above, savvy decision makers will consider potential candidates who are the most committed to the success of the organization and have made the corresponding sacrifices. Who has demonstrated loyalty to the core values of the organization? Who has made sacrifices for the success of the mission?

MARGIN FOR ERROR

Peter pledged his commitment to Jesus:

> Peter said to him in reply, "Though all may have their faith in you shaken, mine will never be." Jesus said to him, "Amen I say to you, this very night before the cock crows, you will deny me three times." Peter said to him, "Even though I should have to die with you, I will not deny you." And all the disciples spoke likewise (Matthew 26:33-35)

Now Peter was sitting outside in the courtyard. One of the maids came over to him and said, "You too were with Jesus the Galilean." But he denied it in front of everyone, saying, "I do not know what you are talking about!" As he went out to the gate, another girl saw him and said to those who were there, "This man was with Jesus the Nazorean." Again he denied it with an oath, "I do not know this man!" A little later the bystanders came over and said to Peter, "Surely you too are one of them; even your speech gives you away." At that he began to curse and swear, "I do not know the man." And immediately a cock crowed. Then Peter remembered the word that Jesus had spoken: "Before the cock crows you will deny me three times." He went out to weep bitterly (Matthew 26:69-75).

After that, you'd have to wonder if Peter was still a viable candidate. But Jesus knew that humans make mistakes, and as such, leaders need to establish a reasonable and allowable margin of error for their employees to learn and grow.

Jesus used Peter's denial as a coaching opportunity for Peter after his resurrection:

When they had finished breakfast, Jesus said to Simon Peter, "Simon, son of John, do you love me more than these?" He said to him, "Yes, Lord, you know that I love you." He said to him "Feed my lambs." He then said to him a second time, "Simon, son of John, do you love me?" He said to him, "Yes, Lord, you know that I love you." He said to him, "Tend my sheep." He said to him the third time, "Simon, son of John, do you love me?" Peter was distressed that he had said to him a third time, "Do you love me?" and he said to him, "Lord you know everything; you know that I love you." [Jesus] said to him, "Feed my sheep. Amen, amen, I say to you, when you

---

were younger, you used to dress yourself and go where you wanted; but when you grow old, you will stretch out your hands, and someone will dress you and lead you where you do not want to go" (John 21:15-18).

As a good coach, Jesus asked great questions to make Peter think. Jesus asked Peter three times to remind him about his denial. Jesus also relayed the sacrifices Peter would make in taking on his leadership position.

FILLING CRITICAL ROLES

Ideally, organizations should have an obvious candidate or a decent selection of candidates to choose from when making critical hiring decisions. As business leaders look ahead to fill critical roles in their organizations, it may seem more challenging than ever to recruit people from outside to bring new ideas and the skills to implement them.

Mark Lautman outlines the impending shortage of qualified workers in the United States in his book *When the Boomers Bail: A Community Economic Survival Guide*. The book explains, "We are heading into a twenty-five year labor market where all the qualified workers in your community will have a job - or two if they want. If your community isn't producing enough qualified new workers and most aren't even close and you are not in one of those cool, hip places that attract talented workers, then you will be out of head room to grow your economy... Your community will enter an economic death spiral that will last the rest of our lifetime." [xxxii] His predictions necessitate a paradigm shift for most community and business leaders. As a result, many companies have added *develop a workforce plan* objective to their strategic goals.

The Executive's Guide to Succession Planning outlines the following five point strategic workforce scheme:

1. Have a Set, Clear View of the Business Strategy.

2. Take into Account Labor Market Factors.

3. Identify and Anticipate Future Talent Demands.

4. Identify Any Talent Gaps and Form a Strategy to Close Them.

5. Implement the Plan.

A good succession plan identifies all the critical positions in an organization and builds a top performer model for all positions, so there is a team in place with capable people to keep things moving into the future.

CHAPTER SIX HIGHLIGHTS

1. Talent audits provide business owners and executives valuable insight on their management team members.

2. Best practices for hiring include understanding how candidates rate in terms of skill fit, company fit, and job fit.

3. Organizational leaders need a succession plan to fill critical roles in their organizations.

Reflection Question: What are the critical roles in your organization?

Action Step: Develop a list of potential leadership candidates for critical roles in your organization?

1. Peter was quick to speak, impulsive, and a fearless missionary for the Church.

2. Simon Peter was chosen to be the first leader of the Church based on his understanding of Jesus' identity as the Son of God.

3. Peter grew into his leadership role by first denying Jesus but later laying down his life as a martyr of the Church.

Reflection Question: How can you follow Jesus' example to help you select future leaders in your organization?

Action Step: What mistakes have potential candidates made and how might you coach them with an allowable margin for error?

CHAPTER 7
Managing Change

LEADERS WILL EXPERIENCE A TRANSITION when moving into a new role. Both transitions to leader and to Christian require an internal transformation to create a new beginning.

The Transfiguration of Jesus
After six days Jesus took Peter, James, and John
and led them up a high mountain apart by themselves.
And he was transfigured before them,
and his clothes became dazzling white,
such as no fuller on earth could bleach them.
Then a cloud came, casting a shadow over them;
then from the cloud came a voice,
"This is my beloved Son. Listen to him."
Mark 9:2-3,7

Definition of transfiguration

1a : a change in form or appearance : metamorphosis

b : an exalting, glorifying, or spiritual change [xxxiv]

Transfiguration is a word that applies to the Old Covenant and New Covenant. The Old Covenant was changed in form and was exalted into the New Covenant.

Jesus came to fulfill the Old Law not abolish it. The Old Testament prefigures the New Testament and the New Testament fulfills the Old Testament. The disciples needed to understand that Jesus himself was the New Covenant. The Old Covenant, therefore, was transformed and exalted through the death and resurrection of Jesus on the cross.

If we put ourselves in the shoes of the apostles, no doubt they were overwhelmed with all that Jesus taught as they traveled with him during his three-year ministry. What's more, they were probably fearful of what was to come. It's easy to see why change is scary and uncomfortable.

Peter struggled with Jesus' teachings, especially with regard to his impending passion: "From that time on, Jesus began to show his disciples that he must go to Jerusalem and suffer greatly from the elders, the chief priests, and the scribes, and be killed and on the third day be raised. Then Peter took him aside and began to rebuke him. 'God forbid, Lord! No such thing shall ever happen to you.' He turned and said to Peter, 'Get behind me, Satan! You are an obstacle to me. You are thinking not as God does, but as human beings do'" (Matthew 16:21-23).

ADJUSTING TO LEADERSHIP

The journey to leadership can similarly be compared to transfiguration. The old coworker is transformed into someone new, with an exalted position of authority. In the ideal world, the new leader perfectly understands and starts performing the activities of the leader role, monitors the results, and moves the followers forward to success.

My Transition Experience

In six months, I had gone from being responsible for myself and my own annual sales production to a budget 325 percent larger and nine employees. I walked into my boss's office to drop off a copy of a report. That's when I saw the copy of my performance appraisal. He wasn't finished with it, but I noticed it wide open on his table. I began to read it and felt the heat of anxiety overwhelm me. My chest was tight. I was sick to my stomach. As I read through the report, it didn't seem to matter that I had been doing my best and working diligently for the past six months. The fact was that on the appraisal, my boss said I was struggling; I wasn't succeeding in my new leadership position. I knew what I read on the appraisal, in many aspects, was accurate, I wasn't getting projects done, hadn't established my voice as a leader, and wasn't managing my time well. It certainly wasn't from a lack of trying, but I was nevertheless coming up short. Later, when my boss conducted the performance appraisal, I managed to keep my composure. Good thing, too, because debating my review might have kept me from the incredible opportunity I was about to receive. While my direct boss mostly offered little but criticism and wasn't personally vested in my success, the boss above him was thankfully motivated for me to succeed. You see, the reason I was hired for that job was that the publisher believed we needed to start promoting from within and grow talent in the company. Prior to my promotion, the sales department had been through a lot of turnover.

Based on my poor performance review, the decision was made to enroll me, a struggling young manager, into a leadership training program. That experience changed my life. I learned the importance of developing relationships and people and a set of specific processes for organizing, delegating, and planning for better time management. I gobbled up the information in that class like a beggar starving for food. I studied it, applied it, and practiced it over and over again, until it became a part of me. Why did I succeed in my leadership position, when so many fail in the transition to their new roles as leaders? The fact was that once I learned the correct processes, I became a very capable and successful manager.

TRANSITION

Transition is hard. William Bridges would agree.

In his book *Managing Transitions: Making the Most of Change*, he addresses something that many leaders have challenges with - implementing and communicating change. First of all, Bridges states that change and transition are two different things. An example of change is when a company is going to switch a manual process to an automated process. The transition component, on the other hand, has to do with the psychological factors associated with the change and, how people feel about it, and respond to the change. The trouble comes when leaders who plan and implement changes do not plan for, and respond to, workers' psychological needs in making a transition. According to Bridges, transition typically has three phases:

1. An ending, losing, or letting go of the old way of doing things.

2. The neutral zone when workers don't have the old way, but they haven't really figured out the new way. This is typically a very unproductive and potentially negative time for workers.

3. A new beginning when the change is in place and going smoothly. [xxxv]

IDENTIFYING HIGH-POTENTIAL EMPLOYEES

There seems to be a gap in understanding how important this concept is in relation to succession management. When high potential employees (HiPos) are promoted within an organization, they were often top performers in their previous roles. Bersin by Deloitte's research agrees. According to Bersin by Deloitte, "A high potential employee is an employee who has been identified as having the potential, ability, and aspiration for successive leadership positions within the company. Often, these employees are provided with focused development as part of a succession plan and are referred to as HiPos." [xxxvi]

IDENTIFYING FUTURE LEADERS

		Current Performance		
		1 – Below	2 – Meeting	3 – Exceeding
Potential for Promotion	A – High		X	X
	B – Medium			
	C – Low			

Original concept by *Society for Human Resource Management.*

One way to identify HiPos is by using a system such as the typical nine-box box grid method developed by the Strategic Human Resource Management Association (SHRM) [xxxvi]

The grid asks senior leaders to rate where employees perform in their current positions. Are they below, meeting, or exceeding performance expectations in their current positions? On the same graph, leaders rate each employee's potential for promotion. Those ratings determine if the employee has low, medium, or high potential. Obviously, the employees rated as exceeding performance goals in their current positions who have high potential for promotion are identified as HiPos in the organization. As discussed in chapter two, a best practice is to identify critical positions within the organization and build performance models using current top performers or other information. Then conduct talent audits with HiPos internally with the use of a valid assessment tool. This methodology enables organizations to create an accurate individualized plan for each employee's development. Examples of employee development could include sending the HiPo to a technical training program, a professional leadership development program or giving them a special project that will build targeted leadership skills. The HiPo may also be assigned a mentor in the organization. Next comes the transition; this is where the growing pains happen.

GROWING PAINS

Bersin by Deloitte's research found that "fewer than 15 percent of companies have strong programs that encompass these areas; most fall short in the identification of HiPos, as well as in the transition and management of HiPos in their new roles. In fact, one of the biggest derailers of leaders is a tendency for organizations to move them into high-powered positions without enough transition support." [xxxviii]

My own personal experience aligns with the research, and I can definitely relate to William Bridge's three phases of transition. Even though I was a top performer as a salesperson, those experiences did not provide me with the tools I needed to be successful in a management role.

Initially, after getting my promotion, it was difficult to relinquish my clients and their advertising projects, because those were the only things I knew really well. As a high-performing sales rep, I felt a sense of satisfaction from the achievements of selling and bringing in the revenue. It was difficult to give up working on day-to-day advertising activities in the field.

So, typically, the new supervisor or manager takes on the new title but tries to keep many of the duties from the previous position. Pretty soon, however, the new manager receives assignments that involve planning, organizing, and delegating. But if that brand new manager hasn't learned the skills to plan, organize, and delegate, he or she will scratch his or her head with no real clue how to approach these manager-type projects. A new manager might take a stab at trying to accomplish a few or all the steps without involving the other staff, but soon realizes that he or she is dropping balls in other areas of the job responsibilities. Pretty soon, the manager will receive another project that requires planning, organizing, and delegating, then another, and eventually he or she feels buried with no idea how to dig out of this huge hole of unfinished projects and has lost that feeling of accomplishment experienced in the former position. When you really think about it, it is quite a logical response, given that the old ways brought satisfaction and success. So what to do? The new manager begins doing more of what is already known - the old position - at the expense of current responsibilities. This is a recipe for disaster.

That's where I was when I read my performance appraisal in the boss's office. I still had my hand in day-to-day sales activities. I didn't have the skills I needed to plan, organize, and delegate, so projects like planning for new publications and strategies to resolve production issues stalled out. I certainly didn't feel confident, nor did I have the respect of my staff, since I also was unskilled in the areas of goal setting, training, coaching, and appraising performance.

LEAVING THE COMFORT ZONE

Even when new managers attend skills training, most will need to spend at least six months to two years applying and practicing the methods before they can consistently apply them to their new jobs. This can be a time of frustration for the new managers, who don't have the confidence they once had because they're working outside their comfort zones and haven't mastered the new concepts. It can also be a very unproductive time period. This was a very negative and unproductive time for me as a new manager.

So if the phenomenon of the new, unskilled manager struggling to perform in his or her new role is so common, why do most CEOs and owners continue to believe that new managers will just figure out how to plan; organize; delegate; innovate and communicate change; resolve conflict; and hire, train, and coach top performing employees without learning the skills to do so? Because it requires time, patience, resources, a reasonable margin for error, and a general willingness to accept that even the brightest individuals are unfinished products. Under the stresses of growing a business and constantly striving for excellence, this can prove to be a significant challenge. But the reality is that becoming a leader is a learned process, like any other skill set. As discussed in chapter five, each role has different activities needed for success. Until a new manager understands his or her new role and the corresponding activities and performance standards, he or she will be unsure where to spend time and what to prioritize. These managers will lack the capacity to complete key projects that move the organization forward while building a workforce of high performing employees and future leaders.

When I began to learn how to plan; organize; delegate; innovate and communicate change; resolve conflict; and hire, train, and coach top performing employees, I made an effort to familiarize myself with the processes as often as possible. I practiced the concepts over and over again, until they were a part of me. This helped get the tangible sales results I was looking for from my team and lead projects to successful completion. Once I learned and applied the concepts, my confidence grew.

TRANSFORMATION

The transformation happens when the new manager is operating in his or her new role as a top performer. In my case, it wasn't as the top flight sales rep but rather as the manager of a team of salespeople planning, organizing, delegating, motivating, hiring, training, and coaching with my new skills.

My transformation became a reality when I understood how to apply processes to my problems. I would sit in my office and list all the problem areas in my department. I'd then prioritize them and assign a timeline for solving them. I kept my boss in the loop and gained his approval to move my priorities forward. I would then decide in which skills to engage my staff and implement a change. I also had a disciplined process in place to set and track monthly revenue goals for each sales rep on all products. Each rep was responsible for presenting a plan for achieving his or her monthly goals. I was proactively delivering sales training and coaching assistance. As soon as I gained control of my time and consistently implemented my managerial strategies, I gained confidence as a leader. Realistically, it took me about three years before I was confident, but once I got there, I immensely enjoyed the challenges of my role. I earned recognition for our department's achievements and received subsequent promotions to higher levels of responsibility.

DEVELOPING NEW LEADERS

Many of my current coaching assignments revolve around this scenario of helping new managers make the transition from worker to leader. I assist them in creating a vision for themselves as leaders. A lot of time is spent working with them—helping them create the road map and crafting methods to get them to higher productivity more quickly. This prevents fewer detours that cost organizations time and money, not to mention lost business opportunities.

New leaders and managers go through the transition of understanding themselves and their unique leadership styles. They also adjust to the new activities that make them successful in their new roles. Many of my leadership program graduates would agree based on their evaluations.

"I really liked the individual coaching meetings! I needed help with time management and setting due dates. I had a lot of issues with delegating and letting things go, and it was really holding me back. As a result of the program, I am more organized and my team is functioning at a much higher level."—M. M., Executive Assistant

"I enjoyed the webinars. I liked listening to others with the same issues I face each day and how they handle them. Very interactive...kept me thinking. I was able to pick up techniques for better managing my work day. I am able to better delegate the work and feel I can trust the people I delegate duties to. I do less micromanaging which frees my schedule to work on other projects."— J. F., Project Field Supervisor

"The program was a great tool to help my team with succession management and to achieve our annual strategic objectives. The group meetings helped us develop a plan to implement important priorities. The individual coaching meetings have helped me to create an organizational system to manage it all and be a better coach." - S.K., VP Sales and Marketing.

The program comments describe how a coach can assist new leaders through their transitions.

THE TRANSFIGURATION

Jesus spent time with his disciples to help them with their transitions. He provided this support in a remarkable way with his Transfiguration.

> After six days Jesus took Peter, James, and John and led them up a high mountain apart by themselves. And he was transfigured before them, and his clothes became dazzling

white, such as no fuller on earth could bleach them. Then Elijah appeared to them along with Moses, and they were conversing with Jesus. Then Peter said to Jesus in reply, "Rabbi, it is good that we are here! Let us make three tents; one for you, one for Moses, and one for Elijah." He hardly knew what to say, they were so terrified. Then a cloud came, casting a shadow over them; then from the cloud came a voice, "This is my beloved Son. Listen to him." Suddenly, looking around, they no longer saw anyone but Jesus alone with them (Mark 9:2-8).

Can you imagine? What a gift of hope and inspiration the Transfiguration must have been for Peter, James, and John as they were transitioning from their old way of life to a new one.

I'm not sure which is more difficult being a new leader or a Christian! In many ways the psychological factors involved in becoming comfortable in the new role of leader or Christian require a type of transformation. Both require a tremendous amount of internal growth and encouragement from teachers and coaches to get through the transition.

COACHING ROLE MODELS

Saint Barnabas is a great role model and the patron saint of coaches. He was an early apostle and encouraged Peter and the other apostles to accept Paul, even after Paul persecuted the early Christians. When Timothy was overwhelmed with missionary work and was rejected by Paul, Barnabas chose to leave Paul and stay with Timothy to support and encourage him in his growth as an apostle of Christ. Barnabas, therefore, is also a Christian mentor and known for his en"courage"ing ways.

Good succession management should include the financial aspects of buy/sell agreements, transfer of stock, implementing trusts, etc. It should also include strategic planning—continuous improvement meetings, implementation of key targets that include increased efficiencies driven through investment and implementation of new technologies, increased sales through new products and better sales strategies, new marketing strategies, and increasing teamwork. But at its core, succession management is about transformation of high-potential employees and supporting them through their transition to leadership.

The Transfiguration, therefore, was about hope and inspiration and guided the disciples through their uncertainty and spiritual change. This transfiguration positioned them to spread the Gospel message to the ends of the earth.

HiPos need inspiration, too. When high-potential leaders are supported with hope and inspiration during their transition to leadership, they can easily create a vision for themselves and their organizations.

Chapter Seven Highlights

1. High potential employees promoted to leadership positions will typically go through transitions.

2. In order to speed up these transitions, leaders should learn processes and concepts for time management, implementing change, planning, performance management, team building, communication, delegation, coaching, conflict management, and hiring.

3. A major component of succession management is the transformation of high potentials to confident leaders.

Reflection Question: What do leaders in your organization need to successfully transition to a higher level of responsibility?

Action Step: What will you do to provide HiPos in your organization with the tools they need to succeed?

1. Jesus spent much of his time during his three-year mission describing the New Covenant.

2. Peter struggled to accept the new beginning because it required Jesus to suffer and die.

3. Jesus provided hope to the apostles for a successful transformation during his Transfiguration.

Reflection Question: In what areas are you struggling in your faith life?

Action Step: What will you do differently to transform your faith life?

CHAPTER 8
Developing Future Leaders

HIGH-POTENTIAL EMPLOYEES NEED ADDITIONAL SKILLS to be successful in their new leadership roles. This chapter covers those concepts and what Jesus did to prepare his disciples to carry out his mission for the Church.

The Parable of the Talents
The one who had received five talents came forward
bringing the additional five.
He said, "Master, you gave me five talents. See, I have made five more."
His master said to him, "Well done, my good and faithful servant.
Since you were faithful in small matters, I will give you great responsibilities.
Come, share your master's joy."
Matthew 25:20-21

It's difficult to be promoted from within an organization. That's why rank-and-file employees need additional support when they make a move to leader or manager. Organizations that prepare HiPos help them uncover their potential and ultimately succeed.

The Parable of the Talents is a good example of the reason it's so important to help HiPos develop their talents. In this parable the talent refers to money—heavy money. According to the Crossroads Initiative's "Parable of the Talents," by Marcellino D'Ambrosio, PhD, "The Lord has entrusted lots of things to us: money, natural talents, spiritual gifts, the saving truth of the Gospel. He expects us not just to conserve these things but to grow them. In the last supper discourse (John 15) he speaks of the disciples as bearing much fruit. In the Parable of the Sower and the Seed he speaks of grain that bear 30, 60, and 100 fold. Whatever labor we are involved in—economic, family, apostolic—the goal should be to develop, increase, and grow what God has given us, for his honor and glory."[xli]

My Coaching Experience

In 2011, I attended a certification event to become certified as a Registered Corporate Coach™ (RCC). Since one of my core values is credibility, I was happy to find a professional organization through which I could learn and apply an accredited business coaching process. A small group of us attended this two-day event to learn the coaching process, led by Coach Carole.

A business coach has a dual focus on helping the individual and the organization. The Worldwide Association of Business Coaches (WABC) defines business coaching as "the process of engaging in regular, structured conversation with a 'client': an individual or team who is within a business, profit or nonprofit organization, institution or government and the recipient of business coaching. The goal is to enhance the client's awareness and behavior so as to achieve business objectives for both the client and their organization… This dual focus is what distinguishes business coaching from other types of coaching. The business coach helps the client discover how changing or accommodating personal characteristics and perspectives can affect both personal and business processes. Successful coaching helps the client achieve agreed-upon business outcomes as an individual or team within the context of an organization."[xlii]

Our small group learned that the coaching process is a dialogue between a coach and willing participant (coachee). We learned that coaching is really about asking a series of powerful questions; the answers help coachees reach milestones, get past barriers, and achieve their desired outcomes.

During the coaching certification event, Coach Carole shared a story about how one day she asked her coachee, "So what do you think you should do?" After a long silence, Coach Carole reminded us she was a type A personality and not very patient. As she continued to wait for the reply, she started to squirm and found herself needing to sit on her hands to keep herself quiet. Finally, after what seemed an eternity, the coachee gave a thoughtful answer to the question. After responding to her question, he continued, "I want to thank you. You are the first person who has ever given me enough time to think things through. I really appreciate you giving me the time to reflect on the question." At that point in the certification program, I realized how challenging the coaching process is and that the WABC coaching process was different from anything I had learned in my previous franchise professional development certification events.

Carole's story stuck with me after the event. To acquire my certification, I completed thirty hours of practice coaching. After the first ten, I had a follow-up coaching call with Carole and told her about each of my coaching calls, what we discussed, and how I applied the coaching process. At one point, we discussed a coaching meeting about a coachee struggling with delegation. I said, "You know, it's just faster to tell people what to do." As an RCC candidate, I knew this was in direct opposition to the coaching process I was supposed to be modeling. Coach Carole admonished me, "Teri, are you going to do this or not?" She challenged me, so I took it to heart and made the effort to trust and apply the business coaching process, including leading coachees to make their own discoveries and conclusions. Certainly, it's crucial to allow time for the process to evolve.

It is very tempting to tell clients what to do, so it's really important to learn the steps of the coaching conversation and to stay in the role of coach. As a matter of fact, the process of supportive coaching is about 90 percent listening and 10 percent summarizing and asking the next question. It's also uncomfortable and counterintuitive. I wrote "Coaching is 90 percent listening" on a card and bring it with me to coaching meetings as a reminder of the importance of listening.

Coaching High-Potential Employees

I have found the WABC coaching process to be a great method when working with skilled, motivated employees. The process helps coachees gain clarity on what they want to achieve, develop desired outcomes for a specific time period and a plan to take action, and ultimately overcome barriers. At the end of each session, the coachee commits to an action step based on what has been discussed in the coaching meeting. The action step should be SMART specific, measurable, attainable, results-oriented, and time-phased.[xliii] When the coachee comes to the next meeting, the coach takes out the sheet from the previous session and asks, "In our last meeting you committed to *XYZ* by *X* date. How did that go?"

Owners and executives should follow this coaching model. As discussed in chapter seven, many HiPos, or new leaders transitioning to new roles and taking on greater levels of responsibility, go through periods of uncertainty and discomfort. If HiPos have a boss or mentor who is also a skilled trainer and coach, the HiPos will be more productive and profitable much sooner than they would have if they hadn't benefited from such guidance.

In chapter six, we discussed Jesus using Peter's denial as a coaching opportunity for Peter after Jesus' resurrection: "When they had finished breakfast, Jesus said to Simon Peter, 'Simon, son of John, do you love me more than these?' He said to him, 'Yes, Lord, you know that I love you.'" Jesus said to him, "Feed my lambs" (John 21:15).

Basic Fundamentals of Coaching Relationships

Jesus was able to coach Simon Peter because they had a strong relationship. If Jesus and Simon Peter had not had the relationship they did, it would not have withstood Peter's rejections and the corresponding coaching meeting afterward. The same is true for any CEO, entrepreneur, or leader. In order for the coaching process to take place, there must be a relationship of trust and respect.

Another key aspect of coaching is that the coach and the coachee are in a peer relationship. That means that regardless of the reporting relationship, during a coaching session, the role of the coach is simply to help the coachee move forward to the desired goals without directing the outcome in any way. Therefore, the coaching process is a strategic dialogue in which the coach asks questions and believes the coachee is capable of creating the right path to attain his or her desired outcomes.

Similarly, Jesus wants to be our coach. Because Jesus was a man, he can relate to our problems in a peer relationship. He desires to have a relationship with each one of us. In this relationship we have the free will to make our own decisions and choose our actions, just like in the coaching process.

The coach's job isn't to judge the coachee's decisions. It is impossible for a coach to perform his or her coaching responsibilities while making judgments about the coachee. Jesus again serves as a role model for us here and offers his divine mercy for us as we navigate through the challenges of our life.

Training versus Coaching

EXPERT CONTINUUM

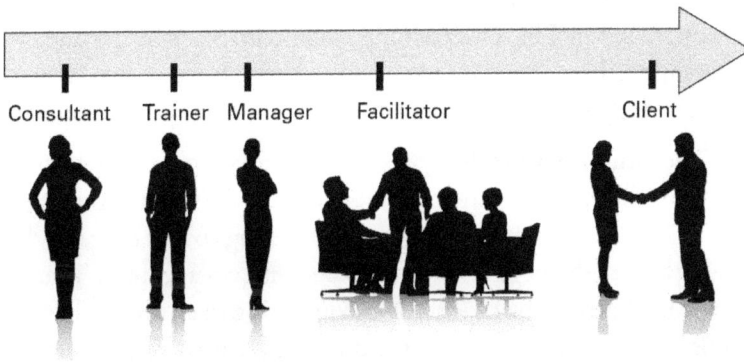

| Consultant | Trainer | Manager | Facilitator | Client |

I use this graphic to explain the expert continuum to new clients. Based on my work in leadership development, it demonstrates how this powerful process works. As you move from left to right, the expert's title changes, as does his or her role

Consultant: If a company hires a consultant, company executives expect the consultant to be an expert in the areas for which they are seeking help.

Trainer: As a leadership development trainer, I wear my expert hat. I am the expert of my materials and deliver the steps of proven processes. Clients expect me to be an expert in leadership development. When I work with someone and teach him or her the steps of a leadership process, I have my expert hat on.

Manager: Employees expect their bosses to be the experts in their industry and leaders in their areas of responsibility. For example, as a manager in the advertising sales department, it was important for me to be knowledgeable about the newspaper advertising industry, sales, how to train and coach salespeople.

Facilitator: Facilitators typically come into an organization in a neutral role.

Client (Coachee): In the coaching process, the client is the expert. When I have a coaching client seated across the table from me, I say, "You are the expert of you, because you have been you your whole life."

The relationship I have with my coaching clients is on a peer-to-peer level. The coachee is the expert on themselves, and I am the expert on the coaching process. The coachee sets the agenda for our meetings based on goals that have been established at the beginning of the coaching engagement. That way, we can uncover the barriers the coachee is encountering in an atmosphere of trust. This dialogue helps coachees work on the specific areas of their professional development that will help them move forward and achieve their goals. This clarity of thought leads to action and application of the training methods.

TRAINING VERSUS COACHING

What is the difference between training and coaching? I asked that myself when I went through the coaching certification program. Honestly, I thought it was a waste of time to coach someone through the delegation process if he or she didn't know the steps. Training is teaching the steps or methods of a process, like delegation. Once each step has been taught, the process of coaching is helpful when the person begins to apply those tools in their workplace.

For example, when I ask most executives what process they use for delegation - one of the most important concepts in creating future leaders by the way - most of them give me a blank stare. That usually means my clients aren't currently using a formal process for delegation and therefore aren't very good at it. Some may say, "I don't have a problem passing along work," and they don't. But what I often see is that many have not used delegation as an intentional development tool to train and develop HiPos.

If I had a coaching engagement to help a leader with delegation, I would first ask what process he or she uses for delegation. If the client did not have one, I would put on my trainer hat and suggest we work through something that he or she wants to delegate. In our meeting, we would cover each of the six steps of the delegation process and develop a plan for the current delegation opportunity:

> **Step One:** Define what you want to delegate and create a vision of the outcome.
>
> **Step Two:** Define which team member will receive the delegation. Assess talent on the team.
>
> **Step Three:** Present the expectation of the outcome to the delegation recipient (delegatee) and ask delegatee to develop a plan to achieve the desired outcome, using the planning document provided.
>
> **Step Four:** Communicate the reasons you selected him or her for the delegated assignment. Describe how it will help in his or her development.
>
> **Step Five:** Review delegation plan prepared by the delegatee and coach for a fine-tuned plan that is agreeable to both parties.

Step Six: Use coaching questions to keep the delegated assignment moving forward when delegatee experiences obstacles and setbacks.

When our meeting ended, the coachee would make a commitment, defined as an action step. He or she would need to follow through on delegating the area we discussed in our meeting. When I returned for the next coaching meeting a few weeks later, I begin, "In our last meeting, we covered the steps of the delegation process, and you committed to setting up a meeting and delegating the assignment. How did it go?" Now, I would have on my coaching hat, because the coachee has already been trained on the delegation process. Now any barriers or obstacles to success on the delegation will relate to *application* of the process. The client is the expert. As a business coach, I ask a series of questions to assist the coachee in overcoming barriers to successful delegation.

CEOs, entrepreneurs, and leaders also exchange hats while developing a HiPo. They wear the trainer hat when teaching steps and methods and their coaching hat when the HiPo is applying the new processes.

That's why I designed my leadership program to be both training and coaching. The training meetings or webinars are typically done in group situations because they're more efficient. We cover the steps in an interactive manner. I conduct coaching meetings individually, so participants can apply the methods to their current problems and talk through the barriers they encounter along the way. I like this process because as a trainer I have the opportunity to relate best practices, and as a business coach I help each person with his or her specific barriers to application. Training followed by individual coaching usually makes the concepts stick better.

APPLICATION

Many have had the experience of attending a training session and coming home with a big binder of new tools and ideas they want to put into place. (Today, it's an online learning portal or electronic document.) It goes on the shelf along with all the plans to apply the material—in all likelihood never again to see the light of day. However, when we return to the office, we are

overwhelmed with the work and e-mails that piled up in our absence.

Taking a professional development program over a period of time helps HiPos learn leadership methods based on best practices, and the coaching meetings establish accountability and help HiPos stay on track with action steps. This dual process keeps the HiPos moving forward to their established goals.

The iceberg visual has always been a powerful concept for me as a trainer and coach for this reason: it demonstrates that we all have more potential than we can ever use in this lifetime. An excellent trainer and business coach helps individuals tap into this potential and propel their organizations into the future simultaneously.

We all need to be challenged. Even Jesus was challenged by his mother, Mary, to begin his three year mission at the Wedding Feast at Cana. "When the wine ran short, the mother of Jesus said to him, 'They have no wine.' And Jesus said to her, 'Woman, how does your concern affect me? My hour has not yet come'" (John 2:3-4). That day in Cana, Jesus began his three -year ministry as a response to his mother's request.

Wise business owners and executives looking to transition their organizations into the future not only challenge high potential employees to take on additional responsibilities, but they themselves also assume the role of trainer and coach.

Jesus took on the role of trainer and coach and challenged his apostles to make disciples of all nations. His main focus during his ministry was to show his disciples what to do and to coach them through obstacles. His Church is still standing today.

CHAPTER EIGHT HIGHLIGHTS

1. Business coaching has a dual focus of helping the individual and the organization to move forward.

2. Coaching is 90% listening.

3. The client is the expert during the coaching process.

Reflection Question: What are the critical projects necessary to move your organization forward in the next 3-5 years?

Action Step: How will training and coaching your leaders help you achieve these critical projects?

1. Jesus wore his expert hat as a trainer when he communicated the importance of Baptism and the Eucharist.

2. Jesus was able to coach Simon Peter because they had a strong relationship.

3. The Gospel story of the Wedding Feast at Cana and the Parable of the Talents underscore the importance of developing and using our talents for the glory of God.

Reflection Question: Which talents has the Lord entrusted to you?

Action Step: What do you need to do to honor God with them?

CHAPTER 9
Developing an Exit Plan

ENTREPRENEURS, CEOs, AND OTHER LEADERS may experience a sense of loss in leaving the organization they created or developed. When Jesus willingly accepted his passion, it was part of a plan. His suffering signifies great hope because of his resurrection. There is another season of life for all of us.

Jesus Follows God's Will
Standing by the cross of Jesus were his mother
and his mother's sister, Mary the wife of Clopas,
and Mary of Magdala.
When Jesus saw his mother and the disciple there whom he loved,
he said to his mother, "Woman, behold, your son."
Then he said to the disciple, "Behold, your mother."
And from that hour the disciple took her into his home.
John 19:25-27

Jesus created a model for succession management because he implemented a strategic plan. The mission began with the strategic plan and the twelve disciples. His foundation of the New Covenant came from the base of the Old Covenant and the theological virtues of faith, hope, and charity. He established the core purpose of the Church as making disciples of all nations to the end of the earth. During the three years he spent with his disciples, he established key targets of healing, performing miracles, and teaching with authority within a ninety-mile radius of Jerusalem. He instructed his disciples about the importance of Baptism and the Eucharist and commissioned them to minister to the people for repentance and a conversion of heart. He assigned Peter as the first pope of the Church, spent time with his team members to help them in their transformation from disciples to apostles, and was both a trainer and a coach to them. He selected specific people with clearly defined roles and gave them the authority to do their jobs. When it was time for him to follow God's plan and suffer on the cross, he had already laid a solid foundation for the Church on earth, and his apostles were ready to carry out the plan to build the Church. It was time for him to pass from this life into the next.

My Experience with Entrepreneurs in Transition

I once received a lead from a colleague about a man who might need some coaching, so I made a phone call and scheduled a meeting. The gentleman was in his eighties and still actively involved in leading his business. The conversation was a mix of excitement about the future and potential business opportunities he was pursuing and frustration about his declining lack of energy and qualified help. He said he was interested in turning more over to his son, who was in his mid-sixties , but didn't trust him enough to let him lead the business. While he seemed genuine in his discontent, he wasn't open to participating in a coaching conversation that would have helped him overcome these barriers and move forward. I felt a mix of sorrow for and frustration with this man: sorrow at his inability to develop a healthy working relationship with his son and others and frustration at his lack of trust.

I will admit that there isn't room for me to place judgment on any of my coachees when I am working with them. I can't be an effective coach while placing judgment. In this case, as a salesperson, I chose not to pursue a coaching engagement with this gentleman, because I work in the area of succession management, and I didn't think he had any intention of ever leaving the business.

Jesus, too, found it difficult when the time came for him to enter into his passion and endure the agony in the garden. He said to Peter, James and John: "My soul is sorrowful even to death. Remain here and keep watch with me. He advanced a little and fell prostrate in prayer saying, 'My father, if it is possible, let this cup pass from me; yet, not as I will, but as you will'" (Matthew 26:38-39).

Committing to anything that appears to involve suffering is scary. This is especially true when we start talking about retirement. "Retirement Worries and Concerns Are a Privilege," a September 2014 article by Robert Laura in *Forbes*, says "Each and every week, a new study comes out that highlights the new or biggest concern people have heading into retirement. Depending on the time of the year and source, some of the most common fears include:

- Running out of money
- Health and/or healthcare
- Stock market crash
- Becoming a victim of fraud or abuse
- Identity theft
- Losing their work identity
- Losing touch with family and friends

While it's just a short list, many of the issues can create a noose around your retirement neck if you let them. Turning a time that is supposed to be happy and joyful into one filled with worry, concern, and worse yet, paralysis from doing the things that will make your life more enjoyable and memorable."[xliv]

FACING OUR FEARS

It's the emotional aspects of succession management that cause the most hesitation. This area comprises all the what-ifs: What if I run out of money? What if I pick the wrong child to take over the business? What if we can't find qualified people to run the business? What if I retire, and I'm bored, and my life is meaningless? What if my marriage isn't strong enough to survive into retirement?

Uncertainty manifests itself in fear. I like how my daughter describes fear in her blog post "The Trick to Being Scared of Everything and Scared of Nothing." She wrote this prior to her five-month trip to Southeast Asia at twenty-three years old:

> "The key is to try to turn fear into a challenge. If something is truly terrifying, I research it until I can feel prepared to deal with it. I accept the inevitability of the unexpected. I think forward to the Emily that has pushed past the mental and physical boundaries and is more confident because of it. That's the best I can do with my upcoming trip. I can plan and plan and plan, but in reality I'll just have to deal with each thing as it comes. I suppose I didn't really need to write an entire article, because I just realized the basis of my mentality on fear can be stated by saying 'don't let the fear of losing, keep you from playing the game.' But there it is, hours of contemplation, all boiled down to a meme I've seen 100 times on Facebook. I often find it humorous that when I come across a really big breakthrough in my own mind, it's usually not some new and amazing concept, it's just some part of myself I wasn't ready to accept even though wiser people before me had been leaving these seeds in my head. It finally blossoms and then you realize all that stuff you thought you knew better just hadn't sunk in or become relevant to you yet. I suppose my advice is let knowledge be your best tool in managing fear, accept that 97% of the things we worry about don't end up happening, and think about all of the times you were scared to do something the first time and after realized it wasn't as bad as you made it out to be in your head. So jump in. [xlv]

As a result of doing the appropriate amount of planning and sorting through her fears and barriers, my daughter was able to move forward and take her trip. That's what business coaching does for CEOs, entrepreneurs, and other leaders who are navigating their unique issues with succession management.

Working Through the Challenges

I find when I work with clients, I get to know them on a personal level. Each one has a unique business and personal situation that requires a customized plan for his or her successful transition. I surveyed a few business people who were planning to retire in the next two to three years, asking for feedback on the following questions:

Q: What do you plan to do in your place of business to prepare yourself to leave the workforce?
A: We are continually trying to "grow" the business further and find a worthy successor. Our practice isn't large enough to simply bring another professional in for a while and then have me phase out, so that makes it more challenging.

Q: What are some of your main concerns as you prepare to leave the workforce?
A: "My biggest concern is finding someone who will take great care of our clients and treat them with the same concern we have tried to provide. My next concern is how do I phase out, and what do I find to provide fulfillment in the future? Happily, I'm still in very good health, so I can continue to practice for years to come, but the issue continues to grow as each year passes.

Q: What is one thing you want to do in order to leave your organization well positioned for the future?
A: We have created a client-centered practice that our existing clients value. We need to market this more effectively to attract more like-minded people.

Q: What is your biggest challenge personally in leaving the workforce?
A: I suspect it will be to find a purpose driven way to fill my time.

Q: What do you most look forward to in leaving the workforce?
A: Travel and experiencing a schedule free life

I appreciated the authentic feedback. As I look for themes in the response, I notice a few things. First, there is a focus on the importance of the business (or mission) and continuing to fulfill and build on the core purpose. Second, there is the financial issue of entrepreneurs being active participants in providing cash flow for their businesses. Finally, there is a need to clarify a new role for the leader that has purpose.

COMMON THEMES

Let's address the three biggest themes of transitioning an organization: financial solvency, sense of purpose, and identity.

To successfully transition an organization, CEOs, entrepreneurs, and leaders need to be clear on the strategic plans of their organizations. In this book, we've outlined the steps of assembling the right people for our organizations, developing core values and the core purposes of the organizations, creating key targets to focus on in the next three to five years, implementing goals, action steps, schedules, and accountability to achieve those goals.

The second area of focus is cash flow. The strategic plan needs to include the cost of planning and the transition of new leadership in the organization. This means those three-to-five year targets need to encompass the implementation plans and budgeted expenses of succession management, which include recruiting and hiring, assessment, developmental training and coaching programs for high potential employees, and duplicate payroll for critical positions for interim time periods if necessary. This is where budgeting is crucial, and financial consultants are helpful. In addition to budgeting and filling critical positions in the company with the right people, there is a need to communicate and make the strategic plan a living, breathing document leaders use as a road map to lead and consistently improve the organization, ultimately better serving the core purpose. The strategic plan is the document that provides clarity to high potential employees promoted from within the organization and new recruits from outside. The strategic plan should be communicated, reviewed, and updated on a consistent basis. It is the glue that keeps the organization together and moving forward.

In down economies, the cash flow and business aspects of succession management can be challenging and a reason to put the whole topic on hold. What is your strategic plan?

A business coach is a necessary aspect of succession management who should be incorporated into the mix of accounting professionals and financial planners. The supportive coaching process discussed in chapter eight of this book is a key tool for helping CEOs, entrepreneurs, and other leaders make difficult decisions, so they can not only leave behind a blueprint for a successful, thriving organization, but also maintain a sense of purpose and identity after leaving the workforce. The five-step process:

1. Guides the CEO, entrepreneur, or leader to create a vision or picture of what he or she wants to achieve for the organization and/or his or her future.

2. Explores the importance of the new future and what it will mean to the CEO, entrepreneur, or leader.

3. Identifies barriers and challenges the CEO, entrepreneur, or leader will face in achieving the vision for the future.

4. Outlines next steps the CEO, entrepreneur, or leader will need to take.

5. Commits to action steps. The CEO, entrepreneur, or leader will need to enforce action to move forward and reach his or her desired outcome.

By integrating the coaching process into the succession management plan, CEOs, entrepreneurs, and leaders gain greater clarity, improved communication, and ultimately smoother transitions within their organizations. This process also prepares CEOs, entrepreneurs, and leaders for potential conflicts that arise during the transition.

DEALING WITH CONFLICT IN SUCCESSION

Last week, I met with a client who is the plant manager at an international manufacturing facility. I spent an hour coaching him through the conflict module designed by Dr. Tim Ursiny and Dave Bolz from *The Top Performer's*

Guide to Conflict. I had delivered this material to his management team and, as he was a valued client, I wanted him to understand the content so he could reinforce it with his management team. I informed him that everything we were about to discuss was confidential, in accordance with the Worldwide Association of Business Coaches code of ethics that I am bound to as part of my Registered Corporate Coach™ designation.

We identified that the goal of full collaboration was to willingly engage in uncomfortable conversations. To begin, he identified his natural style in dealing with conflict. Based on his style, he set a specific goal for himself on how he wanted to deal with conflict. He determined that to have higher levels of success in employee engagement and performance, full collaboration was an opportunity for him and his organization. As we proceeded, I reviewed the five negative conflict styles and four negative communication patterns that can be harmful in relationships. I asked him to identify a current conflict, and we worked through it. Next, we reviewed the strategies of top performers. And finally, he identified a course of action to deal with the current conflict and made a commitment to take action. As the meeting concluded, I asked, "What was the major benefit for you in going through this module with me?" He replied, "I now have a plan to deal with the conflict." As a result of sorting out the aspects of the conflict during the meeting, he gained clarity on how he wanted to deal with it and was ready to move forward.[xlvi] Business coaching and especially the information in the conflict module outlined above is a road map for any CEO, entrepreneur, or leader who deals with conflict as part of his or her transition process.

Chapter Nine Highlights

1. The anticipation of succession management and transition brings about common anxieties

2. Succession management requires the development and communication of a strategic plan.

3. Business coaching addresses the emotional aspects and fears that create barriers to successful transitions.

Reflection Question: What are the biggest challenges you are facing in relation to succession management?

Action Step: What is one thing you want to do particularly well to leave your organization well-positioned for the future?

1. Jesus found it difficult to accept his passion and death.

2. Jesus' decision to accept his passion was based on a plan—God's plan for him.

3. Jesus had already laid a solid foundation for the Church, and his apostles were ready to carry it out.

Reflection Question: What is God's will for you and your organization?

Action Step: What are your next steps to carry it out?

CHAPTER 1 0
Becoming a Resource for the New CEO

THE CHURCH WAS LEFT WITH the gift of the Holy Spirit and many other resources for Catholics. This chapter reveals how outgoing CEOs, entrepreneurs, and other leaders can become valuable resources to help organizations succeed into the next generation.

The Gifts of the Holy Spirit
If you love me, you will keep my commandments.
And I will ask the Father,
and he will give you another Advocate to be with you always,
the Spirit of truth, which the world cannot accept,
because it neither sees nor knows it.
But you know it, because it remains with you, and will be in you.
I will not leave you orphans;
I will come to you.
John 14:15-18

Bob offered me a cup of coffee before we sat down to talk. I was excited he took me up on my request to interview him for my book. In my estimation from the sidelines, I think Bob, a retired CEO, handled his retirement as president of a financial services organization and the succession management process like a pro. I asked Bob to expound on his past forty years of service and if he could give me a few details about the succession management process he used.

Bob started with the organization when he was twenty years old, thinking he would only be there a few years before moving on to something else. The organization was relatively young when he began, with ten employees who had pooled five dollars each. That's the process that was used to form a credit union at that time. That's a far cry from the entity it is today - a thriving institution with nineteen branches and more than $500 million in assets. Five years before his planned retirement, he and his board members identified four internal candidates for the CEO position. They chose to promote from within because they wanted someone familiar with the organizational goals and well trusted among staff. The credit union invested heavily in these four candidates. They were sent to a two-week CEO boot camp sponsored by their trade association, and after two years of training and observation and a thorough and formal interview process, the board selected its next CEO. The new organization leader had outstanding cognitive abilities, a positive work history and demeanor, a strong work ethic, and a collaborative working relationship with the board.

Throughout the following three years, Bob mentored his successor. He spent time training and advising, while creating an environment through thoughtful delegation of key projects. When the incoming CEO brought problems to discuss, Bob asked him to also bring two solutions. This mentoring environment allowed for mistakes, which Bob wanted to see in order to show that the new CEO could learn from them.

Bob recalled a time in his own career when he had made a bad financial decision that precipitated some serious ramifications. He became emotional as he described how his board stood behind him in spite of his error. As his career continued, he made many positive decisions that led to growth and prosperity for the organization, but he always appreciated the backing he had received from the board during difficult times.

TALENT MANAGEMENT AS A PRIORITY

Bob said he tried to hire to his weaknesses. Because the credit union tended to promote from within, every hire from within the organization created a domino effect for another open position. As we toured the facility, he said, "This gal here in this office is really sharp. She came and made a presentation here one day, and I told another member of the team, when a position comes open, we're going to get her to fill it." The same story was true with the incoming CEO's open spot. Bob was already thinking about who he wanted to fill that role and successfully recruited him back to the organization. He stressed the importance of the management team and that the other three candidates who were not selected for the CEO position were still with the organization and remained having important roles. And he ensured that, as they expand and grow, there will still be a corporate goal to improve the bench strength in the organization.

I asked him what he would do differently in his succession management process, if anything. He said he "would delegate more and sooner." That started our conversation about letting go. After forty years of leading an organization, it can be difficult to let go of the day-to-day problem solving. He misses that the most. His board of directors gave him a business card with the title *Strategic Consultant.* When I asked about his relationship with the current CEO, he described it as a father/son relationship, in which he was used as a sounding board for strategic decisions like major acquisitions and new markets. Bob now sits on five volunteer boards to help him with his transition. Volunteering allows him a way to give back to his community and society.

After my interview was complete, Bob gave me a tour of the building. As we made our way through the beautifully upgraded office space in this bustling organization, I saw smiles and waves from many familiar faces. You see, about ten years ago I started working with Bob to prepare his bench strength and was the corporate trainer for dozens of his HiPos. It was great to see most of the high potential employees now working in key roles in the organization. Bob knew training and professional development programs weren't for "fixing" people but for taking high potential employees to the next level.

In Bob's organization, the CEO transition seems to be complete, and the organization has a solid management team in place and is well positioned for the future.

A Not So Smooth Transition

In other cases, the CEO transition isn't quite as smooth. I reached out to Anita, who had recently retired, and asked about her experiences. Anita reported that she had given her healthcare organization a year's advance notice of her retirement. Approximately two years prior, a woman had been hired by the company as a director of another division who had obtained the required license for the position. The organization had already promised this key director position to her when she was originally hired.

"Pre-planning for retirement and notifying the organization in advance allows the company to prepare for a new leader for a successful succession," she noted. "If an individual with the necessary skills and licensure (if required) is not in the organization, that gives the organization time to recruit and train the new replacement." Anita assured that material was organized and available for the new director, while making herself available via phone, e-mail or in person should there be any future questions.

Anita cautioned, "The organization does need to ensure the replacement has the necessary skill set to accept the new position. Many times, as a result of longevity, a person is moved into the new position but is not prepared to meet the challenges associated with becoming a director of an organization." Anita provided training for her replacement to ensure a seamless transition.

Anita also cautiously noted, "Don't assume the individual that has the degree and/or licensure can automatically perform the job. Reference checks and a detailed interview process can help weed out candidates that don't meet the job requirements. If that individual does not have the experience, the organization may undergo a difficult transition, at least for the next few months. Ongoing mentoring helps prepare the new director for the position and builds the individual's confidence to tackle problems that assuredly will come. Staff and regulatory issues can test the new director and the more experience that can be provided through coaching will provide for a successful succession. Turnover is very costly, so getting the right person for the position will provide stability and longevity for the organization."

When I asked Anita about how she was adjusting to her retirement, she said, "I left the workplace prior to becoming sixty-five years old. I am a type A individual with a lot of energy, and coming off a very hectic to more laid back routine was very difficult. In fact, I have gone back to the workplace, even though it is on an interim basis (two months). Being engaged in the community, doing volunteer work, or handling family responsibilities keeps one from feeling useless and not valued. My volunteer work has given me a lot of self satisfaction and helps in maintaining a sound body and mind."

After about eighteen months, the administrator who was Anita's replacement decided to leave for a new organization. Perhaps, if a more intense interview process and more reference checks had been completed, this could have been prevented.

The Importance of Advance Notice and Time for Transition

Both Bob and Anita gave advance notice of their departure and serve as resources for their organizations today. Bob still has an office in the organization, serves as an honorary and emeritus director of the board of directors, and spends a couple of hours a day at his office. Anita is going back as interim director until another CEO is hired.

As discussed in chapter seven, most changes in CEO positions are not immediate but allow for transitions that may take years. Jesus appeared to the disciples after his death. "Jesus said to them, 'Come, have breakfast.' And none of the disciples dared to ask him, 'Who are you?' because they realized it was the Lord. Jesus came over and took the bread and gave it to them, and in like manner the fish. This was now the third time Jesus was revealed to his disciples after being raised from the dead" (John 21:12-14) I have to believe these visits from Jesus gave Peter and the disciples a huge sense of comfort, not to mention the help and direction they needed in the early days of carrying out the mission of the Church

Therefore, many of my engagements with clients and their organizations are ongoing, including the process of filling critical roles in the management team and across the organization and providing training to HiPos to build bench strength. It is an intentional and continuous commitment to people building.

Bob and Anita also spent time with the incoming CEOs prior to their departure and provided support to prepare them with training and mentoring opportunities. They saw their role as helping the incoming CEOs through challenges and advocating for their success, thus playing the role of advocate. Advocates are intercessors and speak out on behalf of others.

The Holy Spirit as Advocate

Jesus gave us the Holy Spirit as our advocate. "I have told you this while I am with you. The Advocate, the holy Spirit that the Father will send in my name - he will teach you everything and remind you of all that [I] told you.

Peace I leave with you; my peace I give to you. Not as the world gives do I give it to you. Do not let your hearts be troubled or afraid. You heard me tell you, 'I am going away and I will come back to you.' If you love me, you would rejoice that I am going to the Father; for the Father is greater than I" (John 14:25-28).

Jesus gave us a Church that is filled with gifts. One major gift of the Church is the Holy Spirit. The Holy Spirit is our Advocate. According to an article by Catholicism expert Scott P. Richert entitled "The Manifestation of Sanctifying Grace," there are seven gifts of the Holy Spirit:

1. **The Spirit of Wisdom** - Is the first and highest gift of the Holy Spirit, because it is the perfection of the theological virtue of faith.

2. **The Spirit of Understanding** - Through understanding, we gain a certitude about our beliefs that moves beyond faith.

3. **The Spirit of Counsel** - Through this gift of the Holy Spirit, we are able to judge how best to act almost by intuition.

4. **The Spirit of Fortitude** - Fortitude is ranked as the fourth gift of the Holy Spirit because it gives us the strength to follow through on the actions suggested by the gift of counsel.

5. **The Spirit of Knowledge** - Through this gift of the Holy Spirit, we can determine God's purpose for our lives and live them accordingly.

6. **The Spirit of Piety** - While we tend to think of religion today as the external elements of our faith, it really means the willingness to worship and to serve God. Piety takes that willingness beyond a sense of duty, so that we desire to worship God and serve Him out of love, the way that we desire to honor our parents and do what they wish.

7. **The Spirit of Fear** - We think of fear and hope as opposites, but the fear of the Lord confirms the theological virtue of hope. This gift of the Holy Spirit gives us the desire not to offend God, as well as the certainty that God will supply us the grace that we need to keep from offending Him. [xlvii]

So just like an emerging CEO benefits from the advice, counsel, and advocacy of the outgoing CEO, the Church and we as members of the body of Christ can ask for the gifts of the Holy Spirit as a guiding compass.

Definition of resource
1a: a source of supply or support: an available means - usually used in plural
e: a source of information or expertise
2: something to which one has recourse in difficulty: expedient
5: an ability to meet and handle a situation: resourcefulness[xlviii]

So where do we get these resources? The Church has a vast supply of resources through which we can seek and obtain the gifts listed above. Some of these resources are as follows:

1. **The Sacraments** - A sacrament is an outward sign instituted by Christ to give grace. I had to memorize that in fifth grade. When we participate in the Sacraments, we open ourselves to receiving grace. The seven sacraments of the Catholic Church are Baptism, Reconciliation, Eucharist, Confirmation, Marriage, Holy Orders, and the Anointing of the Sick.

2. **The Bible -** Personally, in addition to sponsoring a candidate through the RCIA process, attending Bible study programs has been the greatest investment I've made in my spiritual development. Having a better understanding of the Bible and learning how the Old and New Testaments fit together helped me to better understand the whole story. This is a wonderful resource for all Christians and Catholics. Understanding the Bible cemented the importance of my Catholic faith.

3. **The Mass -** The Mass is the highest form of prayer. According to "Eight Reasons to Go to Mass" by Thomas Lickona, "If we give God a chance, He will help us experience the tremendous benefits of the Mass and the Eucharist, the true presence of Christ. [xlix]

4. **The Rosary -** This is also a prayer and devotion. The most amazing thing about the Rosary is that Mary made fifteen promises to those who recite it daily. Ask Mary to pray for you. She wants to be your intercessor and advocate.

5. **Eucharistic Adoration -** "Exposition of the Blessed Sacrament flows from the sacrifice of the Mass and serves to deepen our hunger for Communion with Christ and the rest of the Church... Holy hours are the Roman Catholic devotional tradition of spending an hour in Eucharistic Adoration in the presence of the Blessed Sacrament." [xlx] It's a great opportunity to spend time with Jesus in prayer, meditation, or in silence.

6. **The Saints -** The saints in heaven do actively intercede for us. "Their intercession is their most exalted to God's plan" (Catechism of the Catholic Church, 956). Just as we pray for each other, the saints can pray for us if we ask them.

7. **Divine Mercy Chaplet** - I saved one of my favorites for last. The Divine Mercy Chaplet itself is a prayer and devotion. "The message of The Divine Mercy is simple. It is that God loves us - all of us. And, He wants us to recognize that his mercy is greater than our sins, so that we will call upon him with trust, receive his mercy, and let it flow through us to others. Thus, all will come to share His joy.[xlxi]

These gifts are inexhaustible! In order for us to be gifts and resources for others, we should take advantage of the gifts Christ provided us in the Church. That's why the Church was created for us: so we could be with Jesus in the kingdom of heaven. As it was in the beginning, is now, and ever shall be, world without end.

As CEOs of large organizations, both Bob and Anita thrived in a fast paced environment with many challenges and lots of decision making. In performing successfully in their CEO roles, they developed many talents with the capacity to provide valuable gifts. Both are using their gifts not only to provide support to the incoming CEOs, but also in volunteer opportunities to give back to the community. So in essence, just like the Holy Spirit, they have become gifts themselves. They share who they are and what they have learned with others in order to give back to others.

In addition to being a resource for his organization, Bob is able to enjoy his time away from work not worrying about the daily details. For other retirees, it's the opportunity to travel and experience a schedule free life. The importance of maintaining a purpose and the ability to give back in some way remains constant among all the CEOs I surveyed.

CHAPTER TEN HIGHLIGHTS

1. Most CEOs, entrepreneurs, and leaders provide advance notice of their retirement dates.

2. Smooth transitions are typically made by building talent and "bench strength" in the company many years before critical leadership roles are open.

3. Most CEOs, entrepreneurs, and leaders move into the role of advocate for incoming leaders and serve as a resource for other worthy organizations in order to give back what they learned in the leadership role.

Reflection Question: What does the talent pool look like in your organization?

Action Step: Where can you serve as a resource to assure a smooth transition in your organization?

1. The Holy Spirit is our Advocate. There are seven gifts of the Holy Spirit.

2. The Catholic Church has an inexhaustible supply of gifts for us to ask for in prayer.

3. God's mercy is greater than our sins. We can call upon Him with trust, receive his mercy, and let it flow through us to others. Thus, all will come to share His joy.

Reflection Question: Which resources jump out as most beneficial to you?

Action Step: What is one thing you will do differently to utilize the gifts of the Church?

CONCLUSION

SUCCESSION MANAGEMENT BEGINS WITH AN individual or group with an interest or passion to start a business or organization. It progresses with the steps of a strategic plan, beginning with the right people setting core values and a core purpose. As the organization progresses, its leaders identify key targets to maintain the viability of the organization in delivering on its mission. To keep track of the success of the mission, key performance indicators and results are measured on a frequent basis. Talent management is an ongoing process, and selection tools help with identifying high potential employees. Training and coaching are used to develop high potential employees transitioning to higher levels of responsibility. Leaders who occupy critical roles in the organization supply advance notice of their plans to vacate their roles. They also serve as resources to incoming leaders to assure a smooth transition of leadership and continuous delivery on the missions of their organizations for another generation.

Jesus started his mission for the Church in the desert and avoided the temptation for worldly possessions, power, and glory. He recruited a diverse group of ordinary men as his disciples and demonstrated the core values of faith, hope, and charity as he performed healings and miracles. In addition, he spoke with authority as the Son of God and delivered the Gospel message while challenging all to a conversion of heart. He traveled with his twelve apostles, teaching them about the new mission, and he commissioned them to teach and heal in his name. Jesus chose Peter to be the first leader of the Church and provided hope and inspiration with his transfiguration after he informed the apostles of his impending death. Jesus suffered death, was resurrected, and left the Church with the gift of the Holy Spirit as our Advocate until the end of time.

My recommendation to you is to complete the exercises at the end of each chapter if you haven't done so already. This will give you clarity on where you are currently in the succession management process and help you to identify what you need to do to move forward.

The concepts in this book will take you down two paths. Following the succession management process will help you transition your business into the next generation. Following the steps that Jesus created for his apostles in succession through Jesus will help you transform your life.

NOTES

[i] Rob Portman, "Heading Off the Entitlement Meltdown," *The Wall Street Journal* July 21, 2014, http://www.wsj.com/articles/rob-portman-heading-off-the-entitlement-meltdown-1405983479, accessed July 17, 2016.

[ii] Jeremy Quittener, "The Most Obvious Business Protecting Measure Most Entrepreneurs Miss," Inc. Magazine, June 20, 2014, http://www.inc.com/jeremy-quittner/us-trust-survey-shows-succession-planningfears-for-business-owners.html, accessed July 18, 2016.

[iii] The Family Business Institute, "Succession Planning," 2016, https://www.familybusinessinstitute.com/consulting/succession=planning/, accessed July 13, 2016.

[iv] Bishop Robert Barron, email message to Teri Fairchild, February 17, 2016.

[v] Malcolm Gladwell, *The Tipping Point* (New York: Little Brown and Company, 2002), 38.

[vi] Profiles International, LLC, *The Executive Guide to Succession Planning,* 2014, 3.

[vii] Ibid, 4.

[viii] Catholic News Agency, "Pope Benedict teaches about James, the 'son of thunder,'" June 21, 2006, http://www.catholicnewsagency.com/news/pope_benedict_teaches_about_james_the_son_of_thunder/, accessed July 13, 2016.

[ix] Mark Murphy, "Why New Hires Fail (Emotional Intelligence Vs. Skills)," *The Blog By Mark Murphy and Leadership IQ,* posted June 22, 2015, http://www.leadershipiq.com/blogs/leadershipiq/35354241 - why hires fail emotional intelligence skills, accessed September 16, 2016.

[x] Shahram Heshmat, Ph.D., "What Is Confirmation Bias?" *Psychology Today*, posted April 23, 2015, https://www.psychologytoday.com/blog/science-choice/201504/what-is-confirmation-bias, accessed August 10, 2016.

[xi] David G. Allen, Ph.D., SPHR, "Retaining Talent: A Guide to Analyzing and Managing Employee Turnover," SHRM Foundation, 2008, chapter 2, page 3, https://www.shrm.

org/about/foundation/research/documents/retaining%20talent-%20final.pdf, accessed July 18, 2016.

xii Ricardo Lopes, "Most Workers Hate Their Jobs or Have 'Checked Out,' Gallup Says," *Los Angeles Times*, June 17, 2013, http://articles.latimes.com/2013/jun/17/business/la-fi-mo-employee-engagement-galluppoll-20130617, accessed July 18, 2016.

xiii Marcus Buckingham and Donald O. Clifton, Ph.D., *Now, Discover Your Strengths* (New York: The Free Press, 2001), 11-13.

Disclaimer: Gallup does not certify any external consultants to interpret Clifton StrengthsFinder® or the Clifton StrengthsFinder® themes. As such, the Gallup information you are receiving has not been approved and is not sanctioned or endorsed by Gallup in any way. Opinions, views, and interpretations of Clifton StrengthsFinder® results are solely the beliefs of Fairchild Business Coaching, Inc.

xiv Ibid, 104

Disclaimer: Gallup does not certify any external consultants to interpret Clifton StrengthsFinder® or the Clifton StrengthsFinder® themes. As such, the Gallup information you are receiving has not been approved and is not sanctioned or endorsed by Gallup in any way. Opinions, views, and interpretations of Clifton StrengthsFinder® results are solely the beliefs of Fairchild Business Coaching, Inc.

xv Michael E. Gerber, *Awakening the Entrepreneur Within* (New York: HarperCollins Publishers, 2008), Kindle edition.

xvi Patrick Lencioni, *The Advantage: Why Organizational Health Trumps Everything Else in Business* (San Francisco: Jossey-Bass, 2012), 14-16.

xvii Dragan Sutevski, "Twelve Mission Statements Worth Checking," Entrepreneurship in a Box, posted September 2, 2012, http://www.entrepreneurshipinabox.com/3507/12-mission-statements-worth-checking/, accessed July 13, 2016.

xviii Alfred North Whitehead, BrainyQuote.com, http://www.brainyquote.com/quotes/quotes/a/alfrednort163079.html, accessed July 14, 2016.

xix Charles E. Hummel, *Tyranny of the Urgent* (Downers Grove, IL: InterVarsity Press, 1994), 3-10.

xx Charles Kettering, BrainyQuote.com, http://www.brainyquote.com/quotes/quotes/c/charlesket181210.html, accessed July 17, 2016.

xxi Duncan Haughey, "A Brief History of Smart Goals," Project Smart, December 13, 2014, https://www.projectsmart.co.uk/brief-history-of-smart-goals.php, accessed July 20, 2016.

xxii Darrell Rigby and Barbara Bilodeau, "Management Tools and Trends 2015," Bain & Company, June 10, 2015, http://www.bain.com/publications/articles/management-tools-and-trends-2015.aspx, accessed July 13, 2016.

xxiii "Frequently Requested Church Statistics," Center for Applied Research in the Apostolate, 2015, http://cara.georgetown.edu/frequently-requested-church-statistics/, accessed July 15, 2016.

xxiv Matthew Kelly, *The Four Signs of a Dynamic Catholic* (Hebron, KY: The Dynamic Catholic Institute, 2012), 12-13.

xxv Ibid, 16-24 and 37.

xxvi "About O*NET," O*NET Resource Center, http://www.onetcenter.org/ overview.html, accessed July 19, 2016.

xxvii Michael Jordan, *I Can't Accept Not Trying: Michael Jordan on the Pursuit of Excellence* (San Francisco: HarperCollins Publishers, 1994), 24.

xxviii Marshall Goldsmith, *What Got You Here Won't Get You There* (New York, NY: Hyperion, 2007), 7.

xxix Tom Rath and Barry Conchie, *Strengths Based Leadership: Great Leaders, Teams, and Why People Follow* (New York: Gallup Press, 2008), 23.

Disclaimer: Gallup does not certify any external consultants to interpret Clifton StrengthsFinder® or the Clifton StrengthsFinder® themes. As such, the Gallup information you are receiving has not been approved and is not sanctioned or endorsed by Gallup in any way. Opinions, views, and interpretations of Clifton StrengthsFinder® results are solely the beliefs of Fairchild Business Coaching, Inc.

xxx Jim Collins, *Good To Great* (New York: HarperCollins Publishers, 2001), 32.

xxxi Elise Harris, "Pope Francis: Church grows from the blood of the martyrs," CNA/EWTN News June 30, 2014, http://www.catholicnewsagency.com/news/pope-francis-church-grows-with-the-blood-of-the-martyrs-45498/, accessed July 14, 2016.

xxxii Mark Lautman, *When the Boomers Bail: A Community Economic Survival Guide* (Albuquerque, NM: Logan Square Press, 2011), introduction xv.

xxxiii Profiles International, LLC, *The Executive Guide to Succession Planning,* 2014, 2-3.

xxxiv http://www.merriam-webster.com/dictionary/transfiguration, accessed August 29, 2016.

xxxv William Bridges, Ph.D., *Managing Transitions: Making the Most of Change* (Philadelphia: Perseus Books Group, 1991), 3-10 and 91-92.

xxxvi "High Potential/HiPo (and maturity model)," Bersin by Deloitte, 2016, http://www.bersin.com/lexicon/Details.aspx?id=12845, accessed July 19, 2016.

xxxvii "Succession Planning: What Is a Nine-Box Grid?" *Society for Human Resource Management*, Dec 3, 2012, https://www.shrm.org/resourcesandtools/tools-and-samples /hr-qa/pages/whatsa9boxgridandhowcananhrdepartmentuseit.aspx, accessed July 9, 2016.

xxxviii "High Potential/HiPo (and maturity model)."

xli Marcellino D'Ambrosio, Ph.D., "Parable of the Talents," Crossroads Initiative, posted February 2, 2016, https://www.crossroadsinitiative.com/media/articles/parable-of-the-talents/, accessed July 13, 2016.

xlii "Business Coaching Definition," Worldwide Association of Business Coaches (WABC), 2011, http://www.wabccoaches.com/includes/popups/definition.html, accessed February 15, 2016.

xliii Haughey, accessed July 20, 2016.

xliv Robert Laura, "Retirement Worries and Concerns Are a Privilege," *Forbes*, September 26, 2014, http://www.forbes.com/sites/robertlaura/2014/09/26/retirement-worries-and-concerns-are-a-privilege/#3822455c5d1f, accessed July 19, 2016.

[xlv] Emily Upstrom, "The Trick to Being Scared of Everything and Scared of Nothing," *Wonder While You Wander,* posted on July 15, 2015, http://wonderwhileyouwander. com/2015/07/15/the-trick-to-being-scared-of-everything-and-scared-of-nothing/#more-61, accessed July 19, 2016.

[xlvi] Tim Ursiny, PhD and Dave Bolz, *Top Performer's Guide to Conflict: Essential Skills That Put You on Top* (Naperville, IL: Sourcebooks, Inc., 2007).

[xlvii] Scott P. Richert, "The Seven Gifts of the Holy Spirit: The Manifestation of Sanctifying Grace," updated May 11, 2016, http://catholicism.about.com/od/beliefsteachings/tp/Gifts_of_the_Holy_Spirit.htm, accessed July 16, 2016.

[xlviii] http://www.merriam-webster.com/dictionary/resource, accessed July 16, 2016.

[xlix] Thomas Lickona, "Eight Reasons to Go to Mass," Catholic Education Resource Center, 2000, http://www.catholiceducation.org/en/marriage-and-family/parenting/8-reasons-to-go-to-mass.html, accessed July 16, 2016.

[xlx] "Eucharistic Devotion," United States Conference of Catholic Bishops, http://www.usccb.org/prayer-and-worship/prayers-and-devotions/eucharistic-devotion/, accessed July 20, 2016.

[xlxi] "What is Divine Mercy, The Divine Mercy Message and Devotion," Marian Fathers of the Immaculate Conception of the B.V.M., 2016, http://www.thedivinemercy.org/message/, accessed July 20, 2016.

Nurturing the Flame

www.ingramcontent.com/pod-product-compliance
Lightning Source LLC
Chambersburg PA
CBHW020208200326
41521CB00005BA/298